Learning to
Choose
Choosing to
Learn

ASCD MEMBER BOOK

Many ASCD members received this book as a member benefit upon its initial release.

Learn more at: **www.ascd.org/memberbooks**

Learning to Choose
Choosing to Learn

The Key to Student
Motivation & Achievement

MIKE ANDERSON

ASCD | Alexandria, VA USA

1703 N. Beauregard St. • Alexandria, VA 22311–1714 USA
Phone: 800-933-2723 or 703-578-9600 • Fax: 703-575-5400
Web site: www.ascd.org • E-mail: member@ascd.org
Author guidelines: www.ascd.org/write

Deborah S. Delisle, *Executive Director;* Robert D. Clouse, *Managing Director, Digital Content & Publications;* Stefani Roth, *Publisher;* Genny Ostertag, *Director, Content Acquisitions;* Julie Houtz, *Director, Book Editing & Production;* Liz Wegner, *Editor;* Louise Bova, *Senior Graphic Designer;* Mike Kalyan, *Manager, Production Services;* Circle Graphics, *Typesetter;* Kyle Steichen, *Senior Production Specialist*

PAPERBACK ISBN: 978-1-4166-2183-6   ASCD product #116015

PDF E-BOOK ISBN: 978-1-4166-2185-0; see Books in Print for other formats.

Quantity discounts: 10–49, 10%; 50+, 15%; 1,000+, special discounts (e-mail programteam@ascd.org or call 800-933-2723, ext. 5773, or 703-575-5773). For desk copies, go to www.ascd.org/deskcopy.

ASCD Member Book No. FY16-6A (April 2016 PSI+). ASCD Member Books mail to Premium (P), Select (S), and Institutional Plus (I+) members on this schedule: Jan, PSI+; Feb, P; Apr, PSI+; May, P; Jul, PSI+; Aug, P; Sep, PSI+; Nov, PSI+; Dec, P. For current details on membership, see www.ascd.org/membership.

Library of Congress Cataloging-in-Publication Data

Names: Anderson, Mike, 1971- author.
Title: Learning to choose, choosing to learn : the key to student motivation
  and achievement / Mike Anderson.
Description: Alexandria, Virginia : ASCD, 2016. | Includes bibliographical
  references and index.
Identifiers: LCCN 2015050007| ISBN 9781416621836 (pbk.) | ISBN 9781416621850
  (ebook)
Subjects: LCSH: Motivation in education. | Academic achievement. | Learning,
  Psychology of.
Classification: LCC LB1065 .A633 2016 | DDC 370.15/4–dc23 LC record available at http://lccn.loc.
gov/2015050007

25 24 23 22 21 20 19 18 17 16   1 2 3 4 5 6 7 8 9 10 11 12

Learning to Choose, Choosing to Learn

The Key to Student Motivation and Achievement

Acknowledgments

I want to extend a hearty and heartfelt "Thank you!" to the many incredible people who helped with the writing of this book. Many busy teachers allowed me to visit their classrooms. Friends and colleagues spent countless hours talking over coffee, on the phone, or through e-mail, offering me stories and ideas. A special thanks goes out to Kathy Collins, Liz Olbrych, Gus Young, Pat Ganz, Trisha Hall, Eric Russo, and Margaret Wilson for some great talks and observations. Many teachers in many states have participated actively in workshops, asking questions, sharing challenges, and offering support that helped push the writing of this book. Many of my professional mentors have also had a profound influence on my thinking about choice: Marlynn Clayton, Paula Denton, and Tom Newkirk have inspired and pushed me over the years.

In particular, I would like to thank teachers at Oyster River Middle School who participated in an in-depth study of choice over many weeks, trying ideas in their classrooms, sharing their experiences, and challenging me with questions: Nick Bellows, Sue Bissell, Erin Bobo-Caron, Emma Bricker, Shelby Cormier, Cathy Dawson, Barbara Dee, Jason Demers, Cindy Douglass, Lynn Ellsworth, Emily Geltz, Alex Grout, Nate Grove, Chris Hall, Sarah Keane, Andrea Lawrence, Janet Martel, Susan Mathison, Dave Montgomery, Diana Pelletier, Michelle Pennelli, Holly Pirtle, Miles Roberge, Jen Snow, Beth Stacy,

Diane Tregea, Val Wolfson, and Amanda Zeller. Thanks also to Carolyn Eastman, Jay Richard, and Bill Sullivan for helping to facilitate this work.

Genny Ostertag and Liz Wegner at ASCD helped transform this book from a rough manuscript into a polished text. Thanks so much for your wisdom, guidance, deep thinking, and wordsmithing!

My mother Susan Trask, an incredible teacher and mentor, also spent many hours with me, sharing her own classroom experiences as well as reading excerpts of this manuscript and offering encouragement and advice. Thanks, Mom! You are one of my most valued teachers!

Heather, my amazing partner and a master teacher herself, has been an invaluable support through the writing of this manuscript. She has read essays and offered feedback, asked questions and shared her own experiences, and been a solid and steady presence through this last year of incredible transition.

Finally, Ethan and Carly, my two amazing kids, give me daily inspiration and motivation for continuing to support learners everywhere!

Introduction

My son, Ethan, is not typically motivated by school work. In fact, he is often decidedly *un*motivated. In school his default is to do as little as possible, exerting the least amount of effort required. He is clearly capable of so much more, a source of constant frustration for his teachers, not to mention Heather and me, his parents.

Interestingly, Ethan is, and always has been, an incredibly motivated person. When he was 5, he spent hours "projecting" (pronounced project-ing), creating radios out of toilet paper rolls and pipe cleaners, drawing and coloring snakes and other animals, and building complex marble-run structures. When he was 8, after I read the entire *Lord of the Rings* saga to him over a five-month period at bedtime, he picked up the book and read all 1,100 pages himself. As a 12-year-old, he designed and knitted a beautiful winter hat based on the orange and tan checkerboard color pattern of his pet snake, Professor Quirrell. At 13 he got excited about writing and spent hours crafting stories modeled after some of his favorite fantasy and post-apocalyptic novels. His current passion is working at solving the Rubik's Cube. Having received detailed instructions and algorithms from his cousin, he has been practicing this skill with vigor and can now solve the cube in less than one minute. He can clearly display passion and persistence for challenging learning tasks.

And yet schoolwork typically evokes a shrug, a sigh, and a roll of the eyes. Every now and then, however, something sparks his interest. In 6th grade, there was a particular science assignment that unleashed his motivation and strong work ethic.

Students were learning about parts of a cell. The teacher wanted to reinforce content learned in class and assigned the task of creating a labeled diagram of a cell at home. She offered a few ideas for how they might do this. They could draw with pencil or pen, use a computer drawing or painting program, press clay onto cardboard, or come up with another idea. Ethan decided to make a pillow using a combination of felted wool and beads to show various parts of the cell along with a key to accompany the pillow. Had he chosen drawing, he could have knocked off this assignment in 30 or so minutes and would have done little, if any, deep thinking about the content. Instead, over the course of the week, he spent seven hours meticulously needle felting ribosomes and mitochondria, looking at a cell diagram to make sure he was getting the shapes right and the sizes proportional. His attention to detail was impressive. To this day, he can still point to each part of the cell and name it correctly. His deep engagement led to learning that stuck. Importantly, this assignment also allowed him to practice skills of perseverance and responsibility—qualities that will provide benefits long after the need to know what a ribosome is fades.

Like Ethan, all students are intrinsically driven to learn. And, like Ethan, many students struggle to find motivation in daily schoolwork. It may lack relevance and meaning—they can't find any way to connect the work to what they personally care about. It may be that the learning is so easy that it's boring or so hard that it is overly frustrating. Perhaps the work doesn't tap into their strengths and interests. This book is about how we, as teachers, can use choice as a vehicle for tapping into students' intrinsic motivation, helping them find ways to connect with appropriately challenging work to boost their engagement and deepen their learning.

Choice is something I have been thinking deeply about for years. As a classroom teacher, I gave my students various kinds of choices about their learning in reading and writing workshops, science and social studies units, and daily math instruction, gaining many valuable insights along the way through trial and error. My first book, *The Research-Ready Classroom* (Heinemann, 2006), which I coauthored with friend and colleague Andy Dousis, is all about how to structure independent research projects—an exciting and challenging form of choice. For many years, I worked as a consultant and developer for Northeast Foundation for Children (now Center for Responsive Schools), a nonprofit organization that supports teachers' use of choice as a strategy to boost student engagement. Now, as an independent consultant, I work with teachers in many different schools across grade levels to help blend choice into daily teaching and learning. When I teach workshops for teachers, regardless of the topic, I often use choice to help adults find powerful learning opportunities. This book represents more than two decades of professional learning and growth on the topic of choice.

Choice as a learning strategy is often misunderstood. It is either viewed as something mindless and not connected with real academic work ("You have an extra 10 minutes, choose whatever you want to do") or as something overly elaborate, involving Herculean planning and effort on the part of the teacher (think multi-genre, project-based, end-of-unit synthesis projects). Sadly, it may also be viewed as a relic of a bygone era ("I used to be able to give kids choice, but now we have scripted curricula and standardized tests that make it impossible"). As pressures on teachers and schools have increased, schools' reflexive reaction has often been to clamp down on students, constricting their choices and diminishing their autonomy.

I would argue that choice is *more* relevant and important in today's educational climate than it ever has been before. As students come to us with increasingly complex needs and abilities, they need diverse and personally relevant opportunities to learn and practice skills and content. When students leave school they will enter a world where self-motivation, creativity, autonomy, and perseverance are all critically important, and these are characteristics that are hard to practice in an environment centered on standardization and compliance. When students have more choice about their learning, they can both find ways of learning that match their personal needs and engage with work more powerfully, building skills and work habits that will serve them well as lifelong learners.

Throughout this book, you will find numerous examples of choice in action with students, ideas to try, and a step-by-step process to help guide your planning and implementation of choice. You will also see many references to research and other great work with choice that's going on in the field of education to help place this book into the broader conversation. I think it's also important for readers to understand that this book is based on a few important foundational ideas about teaching and learning. Though these are my fundamental beliefs, which I have developed over more than two decades of work with learners of all ages and stages (not to mention my own experiences as a learner), I have also found these beliefs to be shared by the vast majority of teachers with whom I work. These beliefs should be highlighted here, before we begin to dig into more specific content and strategies, because the best teaching flows from teachers' most deeply held positive beliefs about learners and learning. Unfortunately, too often in education today, teachers are asked to adopt programs and approaches or try new ideas and strategies without any connection to their own beliefs. When this happens, teaching can become shallow and vapid—a series of activities and strategies unhinged from who we are and what we believe.

In this book you will see evidence of these beliefs in action.

• **All students are already motivated and want to be successful.** Though there are many roadblocks that might lead students, especially as they get older, to disconnect from school and appear unmotivated or even unable to learn, I firmly believe that all students are learners. When basic needs are met and when conditions are right, all people can be curious, self-motivated, and successful.

• **It is more important to be a learner than to "be learned."** In today's world, where most people carry a device in their pocket with access to unlimited information, it is more important for students to know themselves as learners and be able to learn than it is to simply acquire information. While content acquisition is still an important skill, the actual content acquired is less important than it once was.

• **Teaching and learning should be joyful.** Students should look forward to coming to school each day. Teachers should look forward to coming to school each day. And when students and teachers look forward to walking through those school doors each day, it should be the work that inspires us and gets our blood pumping. Not pizza parties. Not grades. Not pep rallies. And certainly not standardized tests. The work itself should be inherently rewarding—worthy of our time, attention, and maximum effort.

This book is divided into three main sections. Section I will explore some basic ideas about choice: What does it look like when choice is used effectively, and what are the payoffs—how does choice boost student learning?

Section II will address one of the most common questions about offering students choice: "How do we help students to make good choices?" We will explore how to create safe and supportive learning environments that enable students to choose well, how to help students develop more ownership of their learning, and how to help students better understand themselves as learners. In addition, these chapters may push your thinking about topics such as how you speak to students, how you assess student growth, and the dangers and drawbacks of incentives.

Section III will focus on implementation. As teachers, how do you facilitate choice effectively? You will learn many concrete, practical examples and strategies for using choice throughout the school day. Each chapter explores a different phase of the planning and implementation process: creating good choices, helping students choose well, facilitating choice work, leading student reflection, and engaging in professional reflection. In each, you will consider ways to help students find more meaning and self-motivation for work through choice across grade levels and content areas. While you examine these varied examples, please think of them as inspiration—jumping-off points for your own teaching. The examples used were chosen to offer a wide variety of possibilities, but certainly aren't supposed to be fully exhaustive. My hope is that this book offers you opportunities to come to new understandings about how to use choice effectively to boost student learning, whether you teach high school physics, middle school literacy, self-contained kindergarten, or music across all grade levels.

Before we launch into the main content of the book, let's think once more about Ethan's cell pillow. Although having the choice of how to practice learning the parts of a cell might have boosted his intrinsic motivation, having choice in and of itself wasn't what was most important. If his teacher had assigned the project of creating a cell pillow, he probably would have been just as inspired (though likely many others wouldn't have been). The key is that having choice allowed Ethan and his classmates to all find ways of engaging with work in meaningful, personally relevant, and inspiring ways. This is important. Using choice is a vehicle—a means to an end—not an end in and of itself. Teachers shouldn't blindly give students choices about learning any more than they should follow a scripted program without thought or understanding. Choice is a powerful way in which teachers can help students develop the knowledge and skills they need to be successful in school and beyond—a way to help them work with purpose, joy, and passion—and a way to make schools a place worth coming to each and every day, for students and teachers alike.

THE PURPOSE AND POWER OF CHOICE

This first section of the book explores the many and varied benefits of offering students choices about their learning. Before digging into *why* teachers should consider using choice more often as a learning strategy, it is important first to be clear about *what* it is. There are four key characteristics of choice when it is used effectively.

Choice Can Be Highly Varied

When you think of "choice" in school, what comes to mind? It may be images of preschoolers or kindergartners exploring open-ended centers or having "free choice" time. Or perhaps you envision project-based learning in the upper grades where students spend weeks researching complex topics and designing elaborate showcase projects. Or maybe you think of choice as a classroom management strategy—something students do if they finish their work early.

While each of these examples can be an effective use of choice, there are also many other possibilities—ones that can be simple or complex, short or

| A
A Few Effective Uses of Choice	
Simple Choices	**More Complex Choices**
• 1st grade, music: Students choose one of three percussion instruments to explore for five minutes: symbols, triangles, or rhythm sticks.	• 1st grade, reading: Students study an author of their choice over the course of two weeks. They both choose the author and select the books they want to explore.
• 4th grade, reading: Students choose a good place in the classroom to read during reading workshop. The spot must be physically comfortable and a place where they can focus on their reading.	• 5th grade, math: Students design their own quilt square design using pattern blocks. Each design must incorporate the various geometric principles studied in the unit.
• 8th grade, science: Students watch the same video about Newton's Third Law of Motion. They choose one of three note-taking sheets to capture important information.	• 8th grade, science: Students use clay and toothpicks to construct three different molecules (of 30 possible options), demonstrating how atoms join together.
• 12th grade, science: Students either draw a comic strip, create a diagram, or write an explanation about what happens to trash to reinforce what they've been learning.	• 12th grade, senior project: Students have 11 weeks to work on a cross-curricular research project of their choice.

long in duration, and used in any content area at any grade level as a part of daily instruction. Although there are some common elements of well-planned choice experiences (see Section III), good choice is not formulaic. It is highly flexible, designed to meet the particular learning needs of students given the particular content at hand. Figure A includes a few examples that highlight various choices.

Choice Should Be Used with Purpose

If choice is used as a filler after students finish their "real" work, invariably, some students rush through work trying to get some choice before the period ends, while other students never get any choice because they have a hard time finishing assigned work as quickly as others.

Choice should instead be used as a vehicle for boosting student learning as a part of their regular work. Choices should flow directly out of standards and the daily curricula as well as the interests, strengths, and needs of your students. The examples below offer some ways choice might be used as a part of daily teaching and learning.

- Kindergarten, science: Students choose one insect to study and draw as a part of their science unit.
- 2nd grade, reading: Students are learning about "just so" stories and either read stories on their own, listen at the listening center, or join an adult for a read-aloud.
- 7th grade, health: Students choose one category of drug to learn about: depressants, stimulants, or hallucinogens.
- 10th grade, drama: To prepare to produce their own version of *Hamlet*, students choose to read either the original or annotated version of the play.
- 12th grade, calculus: Students choose which differential equation to solve that is at the "just right" difficulty.

All Students Should Have Choices

Often the students who are labeled as "gifted" or "high performing" are likely to have the most autonomy and opportunities for creative work. They build models, create hands-on projects, and engage in independent research. If there's any population of students who is most desperate for appropriately engaging and personally relevant learning, it's the students who most struggle. And yet, for many students who are labeled as "learning disabled," "remedial," or "low-functioning," what they tend to get is dose after dose of drill-and-kill, rote seatwork. Imagine what schools would be like if all students received the benefits of a "gifted and talented" education!

Choice is one of the most effective vehicles teachers have for differentiating learning in a truly inclusive setting. I vividly remember one scene from my own classroom during a social studies unit. All students had chosen a topic within the theme of Conflict in U.S. History, such as Jackie Robinson, the Battle of Little Round Top, Rosa Parks, and the Space Race. I helped each student create a personally specific set of goals and requirements that complemented the whole-class learning objectives for which everyone was responsible. The diverse class included students who could read college level texts, several with various diagnosed special needs (including Down syndrome, ADHD, bipolar disorder, and several learning disabilities), and a wide range of students in between. Within this setting, all students could fully participate in appropriately challenging and personally interesting work because they had meaningful choices about what to study, what goals to challenge themselves with, and what projects to create to share their learning.

Choice Is Taught, Not Simply Given

Giving students choices involves so much more than simply saying, "Here are your choices—have at it!" Instead, teachers need to help students think about choices before they make them and teach the skill set involved in making appropriate choices (more on this in Section III). Once students have made their choices, teachers continue to play a powerful role—that of coach. And then, after students have finished, teachers help them reflect on their work and the choices they have made so they can get better at being self-directed learners. This all takes some work and effort, but it is what makes choice so incredibly effective and powerful.

CHAPTER 1

The Key Benefits of Choice

Offering students choices about their learning is one of the most powerful ways teachers can boost student learning, and this chapter will dig into why this is the case. You'll learn about why choice can help increase intrinsic motivation and how that can affect student learning. You'll also learn about many other benefits of using choice as a part of daily teaching.

Choice Helps Overcome Two Common Challenges

Students learn more when they are motivated. I know this isn't exactly an earth-shaking statement. We all know from experience that when students have energy and passion for their work and are driven to excel, they can accomplish incredible feats. I also know that all students are motivated. However, like my son Ethan, students aren't always motivated to do the school work that's in front of them. Sometimes, the learning task is so easy that it is boring or so hard that it is overly daunting. Or it may be that the learning doesn't seem to have any personal relevance or doesn't connect with a student's strengths or interests. When choice is used well, it can help overcome both of these common classroom challenges.

Challenge #1: Differentiation

Four students are hunkered down together in beanbag chairs, exploring character analysis through books they have chosen. Although all in 5th grade, their books represent a wide range of reading levels: *Harry Potter and the Sorcerer's Stone*, *Stuart Little*, *Jennifer Murdley's Toad*, and *Eragon*. All students take notes as they read independently, preparing for a group discussion they will have at the end of the period.

A chemistry class is learning about the Ideal Gas Law. The teacher has taught a focused 10-minute lesson, and students are now solving problems in which they apply this law. They have a variety of problems from which to choose as they practice the skill—some are quite basic, some are more moderately challenging, and some are very difficult. Although students choose which problems to solve, they help each other as they work, supporting each other, and deepening their own understanding through collaboration.

In both of the above scenes, students of varying abilities and skill levels are working together. One of the great challenges of teaching is differentiating instruction for students—creating learning experiences that reach all of the learners in a heterogeneous group. (And let's be clear—*all* groups are heterogeneous. Ability grouping and tracking only create heterogeneous groups with a narrower range. There will be variations in skills and experience in any group.) We can feel overwhelmed by differentiation, thinking that we should create multiple learning experiences for any given group in order to meet everyone's needs. The idea of teaching four different lessons and structuring multiple activities for a given class is enough to make many teachers not attempt differentiation in the first place.

One of the main purposes of choice is to provide a few options for students and have them *self-differentiate*. In the reading example above, all students have chosen their books carefully. Each book had to be at an appropriate reading level so they could read it fluently. It also had to be fictional, so they could examine character development, which was the main goal of the learning experience. In the science example, the teacher provided a set of problems to solve that represent a wide range of difficulty and complexity. Students were challenged to find problems hard enough to provide some challenge, but not so difficult as to be overwhelming. Because they're all working on problems involving the Ideal Gas Law, they can support and coach each other, even as they work on different problems.

Understanding why this is so important requires us to examine a fundamental idea about human motivation.

Finding an appropriate challenge. It takes me a long time to pick out a new crossword puzzle book. Standing in Barnes & Noble, faced with several shelves of options, I am overwhelmed. I flip through book after book, scanning the puzzles and clues, searching for a certain difficulty level. If the puzzles have few clues and it looks like I'll know the answers with little effort, the book goes back on the shelf—it's too easy to be any fun. Clues that are so hard that I don't even know what they mean are just as much of a turn-off. They're too difficult. Like Goldilocks looking for the perfect bed, I want one that's juuust right.

I'm also both proud and embarrassed to reveal that as of the writing of this chapter, I am currently stuck on level 245 of Candy Crush. I'm far from alone. Though there may be many reasons that games like Candy Crush (or Bejeweled, Angry Birds, or even Pac-Man—if you can remember back that far) are so addictive, one feature is that they are leveled. They are easy to learn and provide quick success and then become more and more challenging as you progress through the game. This added level of challenge is, in part, what makes them so fun. If they were too easy, you'd get bored and quit. If they were too hard, you would get overly frustrated and quit.

This place of ideal challenge has been called by many the Goldilocks Zone. In the early 1900s a Russian psychologist had another term for this—one that might take you back to your undergraduate days in education or psychology classes.

The zone of proximal development. Lev Vygotsky theorized that there is a place for every learner in any given domain between their current level of independence and their potential for development within that domain. He termed this space the "zone of proximal development" and asserted that in this space, collaboration and coaching, either by a peer or teacher, will help bring the learner closer to their potential (Moll, 1990).

There are a couple of important ideas to understand about the zone of proximal development in order to truly appreciate its connection with student choice (see Figure 1.1). First, this is the sweet spot where significant cognitive growth

1.1	
The Zone of Proximal Development and Engagement	
Level of Challenge	**Student Engagement**
Learning is too hard.	Excessive frustration leads to disengagement.
Learning is appropriately challenging (**zone of proximal development**).	Joyful challenge leads to high engagement.
Learning is too easy.	Excessive boredom leads to disengagement.

can happen. Students learn most when appropriately challenged, so offering choices that help get students in this zone will help students learn more. There is another less discussed but just as powerful connection between the zone of proximal development and choice. In this zone, learning is *most enjoyable.* Whether it's a crossword puzzle, video game, math puzzle, or science exploration, the right amount of challenge—that place where the distance between where we are and where we're trying to get is challenging and surmountable—is motivating. In their book *Visible Learning and the Science of How We Learn*, John Hattie and Gregory Yates explain that "we are motivated by knowledge gaps, but put off by knowledge chasms" (2014, p. 6). In his best-selling book about human motivation, *Drive* (2009), Dan Pink asserts that one of the key drivers of human motivation is a sense of mastery—it feels good to learn and grow. When a task is appropriately challenging, and students meet with success, a job well done and the completion of the challenge is positive reinforcement for the work itself. Because this zone is where learning is most pleasurable, when teachers empower students to choose elements of their work, they tend to settle into this zone on their own. They know their own abilities better than teachers ever can and want to be engaged in appropriately challenging work, so they will *self-differentiate* when conditions are right. These conditions—a safe environment, a true sense of ownership of work, and understanding themselves as learners—are the focus of Section II of this book.

Challenge #2: Apathy

Of course, students vary in ways other than their skills and abilities. In any given class, you will have students with a wide range of interests and passions. Some students are interested in nature, others history, others sports. Some students love working with others while some prefer to work on their own. Craft projects and artwork may be appealing to some, and computer and technology may be preferred by others.

When you can tap into students' interests and passions, they will be more joyful and invested in their learning, and you're on your way to overcoming a second common challenge in schools: apathy. For many of us, this can be the greatest frustration of our work. We spend hours crafting lessons and creating units only to watch students' eyes glaze over and their heads drop. "Do we *have* to do this?" they groan. "These kids just don't care!" it's tempting to cry in frustration. Perhaps instead we should answer with a question of our own: "Why should they?" What does the learning in front of them have to do with them? How does it pique their interest or tap into their strengths? A reluctant writer who loves science fiction may be excited to write a *Star Wars* sequel. A student who is unenthusiastic about learning about the American Revolution but is excited to work with computers may be excited to put together a Prezi showcasing key causes of the war. A student who doesn't always love math but loves to play games may enjoy playing a simple game with dice and cards to practice working with fractions.

Beyond simply connecting with interests, choice can help combat apathy in several other ways as well.

The power of positive emotions. As a middle school student, I was convinced that I didn't like to read. The bulk of my reading experience in school involved assigned books or giant anthologies filled with short stories with questions at the end. Reading was about completing assignments, which I did compliantly with as little effort as possible. Then my 10th grade English teacher assigned a new kind of reading task: Choose a novel to read and share with the class. As a lifelong Red Sox fan, I'll always be a bit perplexed as to why I chose *The Mick*, Mickey Mantle's autobiography. I suppose that for a 15-year-old boy, it had everything I could wish for in a book—adventure, humor, bawdy behavior, and baseball. This is the first time I remember loving a school-related reading task, and 30 years later I still remember much about the book.

Some may argue that feeling good about schoolwork isn't a good enough reason to structure work in a particular way, but as it turns out, positive emotions aren't as soft and unimportant as they may first appear. Brain research sheds light on some of the important connections between emotions and learning. Neurologist and educator Judy Willis makes the compelling case that the human brain is more available for learning when learning is joyful. She also points out that boredom and excessive frustration put the brain in stress-response mode, which effectively shuts down learning (2006). As Eric Jensen notes in *Teaching with the Brain in Mind*, "Teachers who help their students feel good about learning . . . are doing the very things the student brain craves" (2005, p. 77). In short, positive emotions pave the way for greater learning, and offering students choices about their learning is a powerful way you can help them feel good about their work.

Intrinsic motivation flows from ownership. Many years ago I heard a fantastic author and presenter speak about the importance of student ownership of work. He shared a story about a 7th grade student who had produced a poor piece of writing on a standardized writing prompt. He asked the student why he had put in so little effort, and the response his student offered has informed how I think about motivation and learning. It was something akin to "That was a writing prompt. You made me do that. That was your work, not mine." The presenter then looked directly at us and challenged, "Think about your students' typical school day. How much of the day do they spend doing your work, and how much do they spend doing their work? And if they spend all day doing your work, how do they feel?" As Dan Pink says, "Control leads to compliance; autonomy leads to engagement" (2009, p. 108).

Too often in schools, teachers own the work. We create and teach lessons, dole out assignments, and assess the results, leaving students feeling like worker bees, dutifully completing assigned tasks with little power or control. However, when we give choice, we both empower students and help them develop and take more responsibility for their own learning.

An important shift in responsibility. The increased emphasis on differentiated instruction and the momentum of project-based learning and personalized learning highlight an important shift happening in education: the move toward a more student-centered approach to teaching and learning. Interestingly, this movement comes on the heels of the push toward standards and academic accountability that caused everyone to tighten their collective grips on what students did and how they did it. It's important to recognize that these two seemingly very different movements don't need to be at odds with one another; teachers should be able to personalize learning within the context of academic standards. It does, however, require that teachers shift their instructional strategies, and choice may be one of the best vehicles for getting there, for it allows teachers and students to share in the responsibility of teaching and learning. Teachers can create viable options that students will find compelling and appropriately challenging, and then students take responsibility for choosing options that will best help them learn.

Many Additional Benefits of Choice

Through choice, you can help students self-differentiate their learning so work is more appropriately challenging. You can also combat student apathy, helping students connect with their strengths and interests and giving them more autonomy, power, and control over their work, which boosts their intrinsic motivation. These are perhaps the two most compelling reasons to use choice as a part of daily teaching and learning in schools, but there are many other additional benefits that are important to recognize as well, for they help highlight the true power and potential of choice.

- Students engage in deeper, richer learning.
- Students display more on-task behavior.
- Students' social and emotional learning increases.
- The learning environment becomes more collaborative.
- Teaching is more fun.

Students Engage in Deeper, Richer Learning

Students who are given choices about their learning can engage in higher-level learning for multiple reasons. For one thing, when students are more joyfully engaged, their brains are able to process learning and store it in long-range memory more effectively (Willis, 2006). It is perhaps not surprising that I remember a lot more about *The Mick* than I do *The Red Badge of Courage*. Research has also indicated that choice enhances creativity and leads to many other positive student work habits such as self-initiated revision and editing and better organization (Denton, 2005, p. 208).

Also consider how much richer and more varied learning can be in a classroom when everyone isn't doing the same thing. If all students are reading the same book, for example, conversations about the topic will naturally be limited to that one text. In a classroom where students read three novels about a specific topic or theme, they'll have richer and more varied discussions because there are multiple texts to discuss. Steven Johnson, author of *Where Good Ideas Come From*, argues that great innovations are more likely to come from diverse environments. Cities are more likely than small towns to produce great innovations, simply because there are more people, engaged in different kinds of work, who can bump into each other and spark new thinking (2010b). Steve Jobs famously demanded common spaces that would lead to collaboration when the new Pixar studio was in the planning stages. He pushed for a large atrium, a communal space where people from various departments would mix and mingle, as well as centrally located bathrooms which would lead to spontaneous conversations at the sink (Schlender & Tetzeli, 2015, p. 315).

I've seen the power of diverse work time and time again in my own classrooms. I remember Phoebe using a quadrama—a three-dimensional project that shows four scenes at once that she learned at Girl Scout camp—to share about a book she read. Several other students, inspired by her project, asked her how she constructed it, and within the next few weeks, multiple other students used quadramas to share books and present content in research projects.

When all students are engaged in the same task in the same way, there is a limit to how far the work can go. The teacher and the task define the boundaries, and it's almost impossible to go beyond them. When you share more of the power and control with students, giving them more flexibility and choice about how they accomplish learning goals, suddenly everyone can inspire each other, spurring on new ideas and prompting more creativity.

Students Display More On-Task Behavior

A conversation I once had with a principal highlights another important benefit of choice. We were discussing the many behavior challenges that were prevalent in his school: talking back to teachers, staring out of the window, angry eruptions during work periods, wandering in the hallways, refusals to do work, and other such common problems. I asked him, "Does it seem that most of the kids who struggle with behavior are the same ones who struggle with academics?" He conceded that they were. "And do these kids get really interesting school work—projects, challenges, fun puzzles, and choices about their daily work, or do they spend most of their day doing quiet seatwork?" He acknowledged that the latter was usually the case. In fact, in his school it was more typical for advanced students to get these kinds of enriching academics. We both knew the answer to my next question as I asked it: "Could it be that many students are acting out because they are bored and frustrated?" (As noted education speaker and advisor Sir Ken Robinson [2013] quips in his widely viewed TED talk "How to Escape Education's Death Valley," "If you sit kids down, hour after hour, doing low-grade clerical work, don't be surprised if they start to fidget.")

Judy Willis, prominent neurologist and middle school teacher, has noted that excessive boredom and frustration lead to the stress-response in the brain (2006). Students in this state are very likely to move into the classic "fight" (arguing back or erupting in anger), "flight" (wandering in the halls), or "freeze" (zoning out) mode. Research has shown that students with conditions such as ADHD and emotional disturbances that often lead to behavior problems have significant decreases in problem behaviors when they are given choices about what or how they learn (Denton, 2005, p. 209).

Students come to school each day craving interesting and engaging work. When school work is purposeful, appropriately challenging, and personally interesting—all qualities that can be satisfied through appropriate choice—students' needs for engagement are met through the work, making them less likely to seek other sources of entertainment. This isn't to say that offering students choices about their learning will result in a perfectly behaved class. However, students will be less likely to escape to the bathroom, wander around the room, or text a buddy in another class if they are engaged in stimulating and purposeful work.

Students' Social and Emotional Learning Increases

There is a broad range of social and emotional competencies and skills that students need to learn in order to be successful in school and beyond. Students are better able to learn and practice many of these skills when engaged in learning activities in which they have some power and control and when they are joyful about their work. Though there are many such skills, several of which will be explored throughout this book, let's consider just a few for illustrative purposes.

• **Grit.** For many, the first association that comes to mind when they hear the word grit has to do with compliance under duress (think of *gritting* your teeth). I prefer to think of it instead as a state of persevering through challenges within the context of truly engaging work. For students to display grit, there must be a connection between hard work and interest, otherwise we're merely talking about compliance under duress. "But isn't it a reality that we all have to accomplish tasks we don't enjoy?" you might ask. Absolutely. There are many teacher tasks I don't cherish: Making tough phone calls to parents, attending certain committee meetings, and wiping down tables during flu season are just a few. However, because these tasks fall within a job I love, I can attend to them with care and attention. Similarly, students have better energy for citing sources in a research project, editing writing, or even practicing math facts or vocabulary words if it's in the context of work about which they truly care. A sense of power can give them the motivation needed to push through challenges.

• **Social awareness.** When students are working in ways that are personally relevant and allow for creativity and autonomy, students' various strengths, abilities, interests, and challenges come to the surface. Students can see that everyone is different and can begin to see schoolwork through a variety of lenses and perspectives, learning to work with diverse partners and practicing empathy for those who learn differently.

• **Effective decision making.** You can't practice responsibility without having some control. Being responsible, being independent, and making reasoned decisions are skills that many of students need to develop—ones that frequently surface in "skills for the 21st century" or "skills for the workplace" lists. Today's jobs and careers require people to accomplish tasks off-site with flexible hours without relying on a manager or boss to direct every aspect of the work. When students practice how to make effective choices on a regular basis in school, they develop stronger decision-making skills. They grow in their ability to be self-reflective, thoughtful, and responsible people who can advocate for themselves and make appropriate decisions based on a wide variety of criteria.

The Learning Environment Becomes More Collaborative

When all students are doing the same thing at the same time, students are more likely to view each other as competitors. Who can finish first? Who can get the most answers right? Who can create the best map or graph? It's almost impossible for students not to compare their work with those who are nearby when the task is the same. (This is true for learners of any age, by the way. Consider how self-conscious you may be of your own reading speed when you are with a group of colleagues reading an article in a professional development setting.) And once, as a learner, you start judging your own work based on the work of those around you, you have just taken your eye off the ball. You're no longer focused on the learning task at hand, but instead are paying attention to everyone else. Additionally, if you are now competing with classmates, their loss is as good as your win. "Don't look at my paper!" or "Ms. Costa! Lisa's cheating!" suddenly ring through the room as students view each other as competitors not collaborators.

One of the wonderful benefits of choice is that as the work becomes more diverse, it's harder to compare the apples with the oranges. For example, a class is practicing multiplying fractions, but instead of everyone using the same workbook page, students are making up their own problems. As they work, they chat and share problems they're working on, even helping each other as they go. Because the problems are all different and there are several algorithms students may choose to solve the problems, some students are completing more problems than others, and problems all reflect a variety of challenge and complexity. Students are less likely to worry about competing with each other because they're all concentrating on their own work. This allows them to relax, focus on their work, and even be more supportive of each other. Will some students still compete with each other—vying to see who can create the most challenging problem? Probably. And this sort of competition is more likely to be healthy, because it is likely to be mutual and self-induced. As a general rule, the room will have a more positive, collaborative, and supportive tone as the work becomes more varied and diverse.

Teaching Is More Fun

This topic may be placed toward the end of this chapter, but it is far from the least powerful benefit. Teaching is one of the most stressful professions (Anderson, 2010, pp. 4–5), and in the past two decades it has seemed to get worse and worse. The pressures to teach to standardized tests and deal with unrealistic curricular demands make it easy to lose sight of why most of us entered the profession in the first place: We enjoy teaching. There's something truly remarkable, even magical, about being part of the learning process. When students have those light bulb moments or when they become so engrossed in an activity that they lose track of time, it is truly joyful to be a teacher.

Having some power and control over work isn't just important for students. Autonomy is a critical component in our sense of positive connection to the profession and energy for teaching as well (Pearson & Moomaw, 2005). Through finding even simple ways to offer students some choices about their learning, we fire up our own creative engines, reigniting our passion and love for teaching.

In addition to being more creative as we plan, we also enjoy the teaching itself more. After all, when students are more engaged, have more fun, and learn more, we have more fun as well. As I've worked with many different teachers to help them bring more choice to their students, I've heard a common refrain: "This is so much fun. My students aren't the only ones who are enjoying class more!"

Conclusion

Here's one final idea to keep in mind: Choice is most powerful when used with purpose. It can be easy to fall into the false line of thinking, "If choice is such a great strategy, then everything should involve choice." Like any other effective strategy, it isn't always the best one to use. It all depends on your goals. For example, perhaps you want to expose all students to a specific strategy or project so it can become a choice later in the year. In this case, there are no choices because there really is just one option. Or perhaps you are creating book groups based on very specific reading skills that students need. In this case, students might choose in a way that won't allow them to work on the skill you are targeting—you should create the groups and not offer choice.

After all, it's important to remember that choice is a *means to an end* not an end in and of itself!

STRATEGIES THAT BOOST THE EFFECTIVENESS OF CHOICE

In the previous chapter, I make the case that when students are given more power and control over their learning, they will place themselves in their zone of proximal development because that is where learning is most enjoyable. I stand by that assertion, which comes from years of experience working with learners of all ages and in many different settings.

Very likely, however, you were asking one or more of the following questions:

• What if students don't place themselves in their zone of proximal development? What if students choose something that's too easy or too hard?

• What if students choose something for the wrong reasons (especially when choosing based on interest, strength, or need)? What if they make a choice based on what their friends are doing or what they think the teacher wants them to do?

• What if students don't even know how to make good choices at all? What if they don't know what they like or what they need?

These are all fantastic questions—ones I have struggled with as a teacher and that I hear when I work with teachers on this topic. There is no doubt that students may struggle with making good choices, and we've probably all seen it happen:

> Maggie, a struggling 3rd grade reader, sits for 30 minutes during independent reading time, holding a Harry Potter book that she can't read.

> Donald, who is more concerned with what his peers think than anything else, chooses to learn about Ancient Egypt with his friends in a social studies unit, even though he's far more interested in the Incas.

> Marcy seems to make choices randomly and without thought, often choosing problems that are too easy or too hard or taking on projects that she doesn't find interesting. When asked why she chooses one option over another, she shrugs and replies, "I don't know."

> Seth, worried that he'll be teased for being interested in "girly stuff" chooses to take on football as a Big Idea project, even though what he's really interested in is fashion.

For teachers, one of the scariest parts of giving students more choice can be relinquishing control. What if we give students choices and they choose poorly? First, it's important to acknowledge that sometimes they *will* choose poorly—and that's okay. Students can learn a lot about themselves as learners through making bad choices. Secondly, it's important to understand that teachers don't have a passive role when students get choice. Far from it! We must both create good options from which students will choose and help them learn how to make good choices. (We will explore these ideas in greater depth in Section III.)

Additionally, there are many other things you can do that will help set the stage for students so they can make good choices—ones truly grounded in their needs and interests. This section of the book focuses on three strategies that are especially important. Each will help create an environment and give your students the skills they need to make choices that are a just right fit for them as learners.

   • **Create a safe and supportive learning environment.** Maggie and Seth will be more likely to make choices that match their needs and interests in classrooms where it is safe to be who they are. This is the focus of Chapter 2.

   • **Boost student ownership.** Donald and Maggie are more likely to make good choices if they feel a greater sense of ownership of their work—if the work has personal relevance and if they have goals as learners that they are working toward. This is the focus of Chapter 3.

• **Teach skills of metacognition.** Marcy may struggle to find good choices because she hasn't practiced self-reflection and doesn't know how to self-assess. We must teach students skills of metacognition and thoughtful reflection, so they can recognize their needs, strengths, and interests and truly know themselves as learners—and therefore make good choices. This is the focus of Chapter 4.

It's hard to imagine choice working well without these three strategies. How will students take the risks needed to make just right choices if they are worried about being teased for doing so? How will students make choices that are personally relevant if they don't really own the learning? How can students make good choices if they don't know themselves as learners or know how to self-reflect?

However, there's one more point worth making before digging into these strategies and exploring how to foster them, which is that although these strategies will make choice more effective, choice itself is a vehicle for creating each. For example, you can both teach students skills of metacognition so they are able to make choices that are a good personal fit *and* have them think ahead about good choices and review how their choices impacted their learning. This is a great way to build metacognitive skills. This means that you shouldn't think that you must create pro-social classrooms, build a strong sense of ownership of work, and teach students metacognitive skills *before* using choice as a learning strategy. Rather, these are strategies to weave throughout teaching *as a part* of using choice effectively. It is through the skillful integration of choice with these strategies that your students will truly get the most out of choice.

CHAPTER 2

Creating a Safe and Supportive Environment

Few educators would argue that dynamic learning environments require a pro-social context, one in which students feel safe, feel included, and can collaborate effectively. We also all know that these kinds of environments don't usually occur on their own. They take a lot of thoughtful work and planning. This chapter will explore many strategies for building classroom communities that will enable exciting and challenging work to happen.

Two Key Reasons Why Pro-Social Environments Are Necessary

While pro-social environments are important for any kind of meaningful learning to happen, they are especially critical in classrooms where teachers help students challenge themselves through choice. There are two key reasons this is the case: Pro-social environments encourage the emotional risk of learning along with more complex work.

Emotional Risk of Learning

Consider for a moment that the zone of proximal development is a place of emotional vulnerability. It is a space where learning is challenging enough that as a learner, you're not sure if you can be successful. It's going to take hard work and you might need support and help. To put yourself in a place where learning is appropriately challenging, you need to know that the people around you will treat you with respect, kindness, empathy, and support. Whether your zone is lower or higher than nearby classmates, it needs to be safe and comfortable for you to be in that place. A high school junior may choose to "analyze the impact of the author's choices regarding how to develop and relate elements of a story" through reading *Holes*, a book typically read in elementary school. Similarly, to make choices based on interest may also require some social risk. A 6th grade girl might choose to read about a famous football player as part of a biography study, working outside of gender norms. A 3rd grader may decide to write and perform a song to learn and practice key information about American colonial life, taking on a huge risk to sing in front of her class. If any of these students expect to experience scorn, derision, or criticism from their peers, they are less likely to make choices that will best help them learn.

More Varied and Complex Work

There's a second important reason that classrooms need to be pro-social environments in order for choice to work well: These learning environments can be more complex. When students have more choice about their learning, work is more varied, creating a more robust and dynamic working environment—one which requires students to work together and support each other. I've had teachers ask me, "I have a hard enough time keeping track of everyone when they're all doing the same thing. How will I ever be able to help all of my students when they're doing different things?" Quite simply, it's not always possible. That's why students will need to rely on each other more. Teachers must create communities of learners who access each other as well as the teacher for support, problem-solving advice, coaching, and inspiration.

Conditions to Nurture

Creating classrooms where students can engage in robust learning requires thoughtful work on the part of the teacher. We can't simply cross our fingers and hope that we get a class that works well together. As a colleague of mine likes to say, "Hope is not a classroom management strategy." Instead, we need to think about the characteristics students need to exhibit and then craft learning environments where those characteristics can be practiced. As Figure 2.1 demonstrates, there are a few pro-social characteristics that are especially important to nurture:

- **Safety.** Students need to feel safe enough to take risks inherent in choice.
- **Inclusion.** Students need to feel a sense of positive connection to the class: to know each other, be known, and be valued for their strengths and positive attributes. This enables students to tap into each other and share ideas that allow work to be more dynamic and rigorous.
- **Collaboration.** Students must be able to work with each other well. A classroom with choice offers more varied partner and grouping opportunities, and students need the necessary skills to work together effectively.

A challenge of writing this chapter was that it required a linear examination of nonlinear content. After all, a book is read (generally) in a front-to-back, beginning-to-end manner. However, these characteristics all flow together and connect in a nonlinear fashion. Inclusion and collaboration are essential to a sense of safety. It would be impossible to have effective collaboration without safety and inclusion. Keep this in mind as you read. Any of the strategies suggested could be tried in a variety of orders and ways. You know your students best. Look at their needs, their strengths, and the overall tone of your room, and decide what ideas are most important to help your students make the choices necessary to engage in authentic, dynamic, and high-quality learning.

2.1

Purposeful Relationship Building

One of the most critical elements of a positive social learning environment is the establishment of positive relationships. Students must feel known and connected, both with teachers and peers. If one of the hallmarks of real learning (which choice helps to create) is that it requires emotional vulnerability, then it's clear that students must trust those around them, teachers and students alike. Building positive relationships—both with and among your students—must therefore be considered one of your most important tasks as teachers.

Nurturing Teacher-Student Relationships

There is compelling evidence that shows it is immensely important for students to trust their teachers. Various research studies have shown connections between how students feel they are treated at school and achievement, motivation, and even physical and psychological health (Hattie & Yates, 2014, pp. 26–27). In a classroom where some of the responsibility for learning shifts to the students, it becomes even more important that they feel safe and comfortable with their teachers. Students will better be able to take real learning risks when they feel safe, and they will better be able to seek out the help they need when they are in the zone of proximal development—that learning space where coaching and support is needed to learn.

There are, of course, many ways you can develop positive relationships with your students. The following list may serve as a good starting point—some ideas to get you going in the right direction.

• **Get to know students.** Ask students about their interests and activities outside of school. Ask about their friends and families. Keep a simple file where you can jot down one or two things about each student, and then make sure to chat with students about that information.

• **Share about yourself.** Share about your interests, your family, and yourself as a learner. Blend in little tidbits of personal information as you teach, letting your students know you better.

• **Be your best self.** Smile. Be warm, approachable, and kind. Be someone worthy of trust and respect.

It is important to note here that in addition to helping students develop a sense of trust and safety, building relationships also helps you know what kinds of choices you might offer, for the better you know your students, the better able you are to offer options that fit them well.

Supporting Positive Peer Relationships

Though many students will have strong friendships with some classmates and may struggle socially with others, it is important that all students learn to work with a wide variety of classmates. There may be times when students choose to work alone or with a partner to practice a skill, or they might get to choose a novel to read as part of a literature study group. In a classroom where students don't feel safe or comfortable working with everyone else, they may make choices motivated by who they want to work with (or avoid) instead of what they will do. Because you want students to make choices based on their needs as learners and not solely on who they want to work with, students need to know each other well enough that they can comfortably work with many of their classmates. The intense pressures to teach as much content as quickly as possible can make it feel hard to find the time to build relationships in a classroom, but I argue that there isn't time *not* to. Here are a few important ideas to help guide this work.

Relationship building must be planned and taught. It is too important to leave the development of positive peer interactions to chance. We should consider the kinds of interactions and relationships we want to see exhibited in our classrooms and plan and teach accordingly, just as we do with academic goals and skills.

High social expectations lead to high academic outcomes. Students deserve to be accepted by each other, not simply tolerated. Students deserve to have friendly interactions with others throughout the school day. The adults in a school should have no tolerance for snarky student interactions, mean name-calling, or exclusionary behavior. All students, not just the best-dressed, most athletic, most socially powerful ones, need to feel accepted. And when they do, they will be more connected with school and will learn more.

Relationship building is ongoing. Building strong relationships must be a priority at the beginning of the year. However, this work doesn't end in October.

You must make collegial and positive interactions and personal connections part of the daily work of classroom life throughout the year.

Here are a few simple strategies that can help you nurture positive peer relationships in your classrooms:

• **Add social components to academic tasks.** As students begin to work on a collaborative activity, begin with a warm-up to help students connect personally. "Okay, everyone. Before you get going on your science task, you're going to warm up with a fun challenge. You have two minutes to see how many similarities you can find that all group members share!"

• **Mix partners and groups frequently.** Assign or designate partners, and keep mixing it up. When everyone works with everyone else, students learn to respect and value peers outside of their immediate friendship groups. The tone of the room becomes more inclusive and supportive.

• **For project work, help divvy up tasks.** It's too easy for assertive or typically high achieving students to take over while more reticent students take a back seat when group work is being parsed out; one does the research, one does the writing, the third colors the poster. Make sure that all group members have valuable and important work to contribute to the group.

• **Use daily rituals to build community.** Many elementary classrooms begin their day with students meeting together to connect, share, and play. Many middle and high school schedules include an advisory period in which students connect with a small peer group and caring adult to connect and support each other. Daily rituals like this help build solid communities that support academic risk-taking all day long.

Firm and Respectful Discipline

Discipline systems can either help create safe and supportive environments or diminish them. Are discipline and management techniques clear, reliable, and respectful of students and adults? If so, students will settle into school, knowing that the adults in charge will maintain an orderly and safe environment. This will free them up to make choices that are truly personally relevant instead of making choices that seem safe or popular.

Discipline systems in schools often fall into two very different but equally problematic categories. In some schools, discipline is overly authoritarian and punitive. Adults wield all of the power and control, and fear, intimidation, bribes, and shame are tools used to coerce students into appropriate behavior. In others, discipline is loose and weak. Adults hope that kids will behave appropriately, leading to frequent limit-testing and a constant current of mild disrespect. Both of these systems create a climate of uneasiness that will make students less likely to take academic risks.

Ideally, adults have a strong voice of authority but share power and control with students. Teachers believe that students want to be positive and productive members of a class and also recognize that all kids make mistakes and will need coaching and guidance. Students are held to high standards of respectful behavior and are redirected kindly and firmly by teachers who empathize with students who struggle. Recognizing that the goal of effective discipline is the development of self-discipline, students are taught strategies and skills to become more responsible, respectful, and caring students. This sets a classroom tone where students know that it is safe to choose options that are truly a good fit and where struggles and mistakes will be met with support and empathy (see Figure 2.2).

2.2
Discipline Practices to Avoid and Try

Instead of . . .	Try . . .
• **Public systems.** Names on the board, red/yellow/green lights, and so on make students' discipline challenges public, often causing shame, anxiety, or rebellion.	• **Collaborative rules.** Create rules together with your students, asking them for input into the kinds of common expectations that will help create a caring community where kids can do great work.
• **Yelling.** When adults yell in anger or frustration, they have lost control and are trying to intimidate students. Yelling should be reserved for stopping a behavior that is unsafe (like a student about to punch another).	• **Modeling.** Teach students positive expectations, have them practice, and repeat as needed.
• **Punishing.** The notion that kids will behave well only when made to feel bad is nonsensical. This is one of the most commonly used discipline practices, and if it worked, we'd know by now.	• **Respectful consequences.** Did someone do a sloppy job on a piece of work? They should redo it. Did someone say something mean to someone else? They should make amends. Keep consequences simple and about fixing mistakes, not paying for them.

For a more thorough examination of effective discipline techniques, consider exploring *Rules in School* (K-6) (Brady, Forton, & Porter, 2010) and *Getting Classroom Management Right* (7-12) (Lieber, 2009).

Language: The Classroom Tone-Setter

As Haim Ginott noted many years ago, teachers have immense influence over the tone and feel of a classroom: "I have come to the frightening conclusion that I am the decisive element. It is my personal approach that creates the climate. It is my daily mood that makes the weather. I possess tremendous power to make life miserable or joyous. I can be a tool of torture or an instrument of inspiration, I can humiliate or humor, hurt or heal. In all situations, it is my response that decides whether a crisis is escalated or de-escalated, and a person is humanized or de-humanized" (1972, p. 15).

Language is the primary vehicle for setting the tone of the room. If a teacher's language is kind, sincere, supportive, and professional, students feel safe. They also take their cue about how to treat others by how teachers talk to them. If a teacher is sarcastic, demeaning, or abrasive, they will quickly follow suit, making inclusive and collaborative work almost impossible and making students less likely to choose work that is appropriately challenging or based on their own unique needs and interests.

If you want a classroom that feels more supportive and safe, language should emphasize collaboration over competition, quality over quantity, and self-reflection over comparison (see Figure 2.3).

Language is so nuanced. It is greatly influenced by tone of voice, cultural norms, body language, relationships, and even the current mood of the listener. This can make it hard when examining your own language to decide when language is simply direct or overly harsh, ironic or sarcastic, friendly or overly sentimental. Here's a bellwether you might try. Think about the language you are analyzing and then shift the setting from the classroom to a staff meeting. How would it sound if a principal used that same language at a staff meeting? Would you, as a teacher, feel safe, included, and collaborative? Would you be more or less likely to take a risk as a result of that language?

2.3 Language to Avoid and to Try		
Context	**Instead of . . .**	**Try . . .**
A class is about to brainstorm possible choices for an upcoming unit.	"Who has a great idea to share?" (Worrying their idea isn't **great**, some students may not volunteer an idea.)	"Who has an idea to share?"
Students are about to choose an article about the Amazon Rainforest to read.	"This first article is really easy, and this third article is really challenging." (Some kids may choose one that's too hard in an attempt to impress.)	"Look through each of these articles and decide which will be the best fit for you. They all have great information in them!"
A few students are supposed to be cleaning up a work space. Only one of them is.	Look at how well Markus is cleaning up! (Markus may feel embarrassed, his peers resentful.)	"Remember, everyone should be cleaning up right now."
Students are finding the area of various triangles. Jeannie is staring out the window.	"Jeannie? You've only done three problems? Most kids have already done six or seven . . . you need to speed up!" (Emphasizes speed and comparison, may foster anxiety or feelings of inadequacy.)	"Jeannie, refocus. Let me know if you need any help."

An Egalitarian Classroom

All students in a classroom should have equal access to high-quality choices. When some students don't have materials that others have, they may feel devalued or resentful. When some students are called on frequently and others aren't, when some are held to high standards and others aren't, when some are clearly more connected with the teacher than others, the learning environment feels competitive rather than collaborative and exclusive rather than inclusive. Some students will be less likely or able to choose well.

Names Are Valued and Used

It's surprising how a simple practice such as using students' names can have such a profound impact. I was talking with a middle school student recently about his favorite teachers. He generally liked most of his teachers, but when he got to one, he rolled his eyes. "Ms. B never uses my name. She does it all the time. She calls a bunch of us 'sweetie' and 'honey.' I mean, *come on*, we're her students not her grandkids!" He clearly felt devalued and disrespected by being called "sweetie," but I picked up on something else in his gripe. It sounds like this teacher doesn't refer to all of the students in this way, just some. Could it be that she doesn't know all of her students' names? Or could it be that she enjoys some more than others? Either way, any sense of positive community in the classroom will erode if some students are called by name and others aren't. Make sure to call students by their preferred names.

Likewise, make sure students use each other's names. Don't allow nicknames that feel disrespectful or overly playful to be used in class as this can have a negative impact on some students' sense of belonging and significance. Require all students to wear name tags at the beginning of the year until everyone has learned each other's names. Keep name tags on hand for when new students or guest teachers join the class.

All Students Get High-Quality Attention from the Teacher

Do you call on girls as often as boys? Are there certain students you gravitate toward and spend extra time with and others with whom you have a harder time connecting? Of course, it would be impossible to spend exactly the same amount and quality of time with each of your students. Yet, try to be conscious of the message that your interactions with students sends. If you call on certain kids to answer high-level questions and not others, what message has been sent? If some students hear their names connected with negative behaviors more than academic work, what might they (and others) assume? Try recording a lesson using a phone or tablet and then listening for patterns of interactions. Or you might use a class list at the end of a lesson to check off students with whom you interacted. These are just two ways to collect some information about your interactions with students as you work toward building more egalitarian classrooms.

All Students Have Access to the Same Materials

What is the message that is sent in a classroom if some students have access to high-quality supplies and others don't? How would you feel as a learner if certain choices were available to others, but not to you? When students can bring in technology or supplies from home and those resources aren't available to everyone, it's easy for some to feel resentful.

I had a protocol about this in my classroom. Any supply or material that was brought into the room had to be available for anyone. If a student had a special pack of markers, everyone had to be able to use them. If only he (and his three closest friends) were going to be able to use them, they stayed home. If all students needed three-ring binders for portfolios, I would purchase a class set with school money, rather than requiring students to bring in their own, which was a questionable school practice that would result in some students having beautiful new binders with special flaps and folders while others brought in banged up used ones. The overall feel and tone of the classroom is more important than individual students' desire to have the best stuff.

A Room Designed for Pro-Social Interactions

Have you ever noticed how much the décor of a space affects how you feel there? Consider the importance of lighting, artwork, and plants in a fine restaurant or natural light and attractive displays in a nice store. If you want your learning environment to feel safe and supportive, you can craft a space that will encourage those characteristics.

A Cozy Feel

Think about a place you love to do reflective work—something like reading, writing, or planning. Perhaps there's a café nearby with comfy seats and a friendly atmosphere. Or maybe you love a spot at your local library; there's a table near a window with great natural light. Whatever the space is, I bet I can guess some of its key characteristics: the lighting is pleasant, the colors are soothing and warm, the décor is inviting, the space is neat and clean, and the staff or other people there are helpful and respectful. What if when creating your classroom space, instead of designing a classroom, you instead design a space where great work can happen? Create a classroom where students feel safe and ready to work with others and one you will look forward to coming to each day. Make sure that in this space, there are a variety of places where students might work, depending on their preferences and the demands of their learning: comfy solo spots for quiet individual work; tables for small-group work; and spaces that can easily be reconfigured to suit the needs of students and their work.

Spaces That Foster Sharing and Collaboration

Kaylee is designing a project to highlight key figures from the French Revolution, the world event she chose to study as a part of a unit on The Age of Revolutions (1750–1914). Using oak tag, she is creating a three-dimensional display that will allow her to show several different events at once. Brian, working on a laptop at Kaylee's table, is intrigued and asks her about it. He is designing a PowerPoint slideshow to highlight characteristics of Joshua Lawrence Chamberlain, colonel of the 20th Maine regiment from the Battle of Gettysburg. The idea of showing multiple scenes inspires his own thinking. He decides to craft a four-quadrant slide to highlight several characteristics at once.

In the TED talk "Where Good Ideas Come From," Steven Johnson talks about the importance of the coffee house in the flowering of ideas during the Enlightenment. With comfortable furniture facing together and a cozy atmosphere, "It was a space where people would get together from different backgrounds, different fields of expertise, and share" (2010a). He goes on to cite Matt Ridley, "It was a place where ideas could have sex" (2010a). Not, perhaps, a metaphor to share with students, but one that rings true of collaborative classrooms. Sometimes, the best ideas happen when two people share ideas that inspire something new. My friend and colleague Andy Dousis refers to this as "collateral learning." Though not necessarily planned, it's the unexpected learning that happens within the context of planned work that is truly inspiring and one of the great benefits of offering students more choice in their learning.

In a classroom designed for collaboration, the general seating arrangement is one in which students can easily collaborate and share with each other. Pods of desks and table groups send the message that students will work together, whereas desks in rows or a horseshoe typically mean that the teacher is the center of attention. The classic Harkness table circle arrangement for high school and college class discussions sends the message that students will look at and value each other as they discuss, as opposed to all students facing the teacher.

It's important to recognize, though, that in a classroom designed for collaboration, students will talk more. A lecture-based classroom is best served by students sitting in rows. So, if students face each other, they need to spend more time talking with each other and less time listening to teachers. In addition to increasing the amount of work time they have for the choices they select, make sure to also blend in other interactions to lessons and activities. Brief table talks and partner chats can help students converse productively throughout the day, giving them more practice at collaboration and helping talk stay focused on learning.

Making Flexible Seating Safe

The tone of a classroom improves when students no longer view specific real estate as theirs (*my* seat, *my* table, *my* chair) but instead consider the whole room as shared space (*our* seats, *our* tables, *our* chairs).

• **Designate seats.** Allowing students to have free choice of seating may work in some instances, especially later in the year. Most of the time, however, it's best to designate where students will work depending on the choices they have made or the groups you want them to be in. "Jamal, Destiny, Sarah, and Richard—head to this table to work on finding least common denominators. Micah, Diamond, Jesse, and Roman, head to this table because you decided to practice converting fractions to decimals." This creates a sense of safety for students and helps them get used to working with many different classmates, not just their go-to friends. When grouped by choice, students are then able to support and coach each other as they work.

• **Label work areas.** Labeling table groups makes it easier to direct students to work spaces. In younger grades, you might label groups by color or animal name. In upper grades you might designate tables with sports teams or local colleges and universities ("If you are working on revising or editing your writing and will need to talk with others, head to Boston College or Tufts. If you are working on a draft and will need quiet concentration, go to Northeastern, Brandeis, or Boston University") or content specific labels ("If you are working on Lab X, meet at the Niels Bohr or Stephen Hawking stations. Those of you trying Lab Y, join together at the Max Born or Isaac Newton stations").

• **Have a go-to seat.** Having a place to go to begin the day, a particular class, or a lesson gives students a safe anchor. Then they can move to the appropriate place to work based on their choice once they get going.

Rethinking Competition

In my first year teaching, I had students play a game called Around the World to help them practice math facts. The class sat in a circle. Two students would stand, and I would fire a math fact at them: "7x6!" The first student to respond correctly would win and advance to the next person in the circle. The loser sat back down. The object of the game was to see how far around the circle students could travel. My intentions were good. I was trying to make practicing math facts, a task which often feels tedious, more fun. Deceived by the enthusiasm of the few students who loved the game (incidentally, the ones who had already mastered their facts), it took me a while to recognize the trouble with this activity. Many students in fact did not like the game. They quietly endured it, knowing they weren't going to get very far. Some folded their arms stoically and glared at the floor, preferring to shut down rather than look stupid. Importantly, because of the competitive nature of the game, there was little positive payoff for learning. Students who already knew their facts got the most practice and felt superior. Students who struggled practiced less and had their shortcoming highlighted publicly, reinforcing their anxiety about math.

Competitions like these can foster resentment in a classroom, damaging student relationships and making it harder for students to work well together. Students who often win may be teased for being too smart (a defense mechanism on the part of students who feel diminished by losing), and students who win may look down on peers who struggle, no longer viewing them as worthy of collaboration. Additionally, competitive atmospheres may lead some students to choose tasks that are too easy (trying not to make mistakes) or too hard (wanting to look smart). So instead, replace competitive activities with ones that are fun and safe for all.

Some practices don't seem competitive on the surface, but upon closer inspection clearly have students comparing themselves to (and competing with) others. Public discipline systems (names on the board, red/yellow/green light cards, etc.), posting charts showing which students have completed assignments or met benchmark standards, sharing some students' work as "best" examples for others to emulate, having students correct and score each other's homework, or passing back tests in the order of grades achieved are all examples of practices that encourage students to compare themselves to others and should be avoided.

A Place for Competition

Not all competition is bad, of course. In fact, I love to compete. I was a competitive swimmer from childhood through college. Now, I run 5K road races, play Words with Friends on a daily basis, and use my FitBit friends group as daily motivation for getting in a few extra steps. Many students also thrive on competition, so let's consider a couple of ideas for using competition effectively when using choice.

• **Students may choose competition.** Consider offering competitive options for students who enjoy it. For example, one choice for ways to practice mental math can be a game called Race the Calculator. Two students get a problem. One solves it in her head while the other races her using a calculator. Students who prefer to practice in a non-competitive way can practice problems with flash cards. In another instance, students might have two options for practicing words with an "ea" vowel combination. They can either look through their reading books for examples (noncompetitive) or play a competitive Boggle game with a small group (using teacher-created sheets with "ea" combinations). Giving students both competitive and noncompetitive options allows those who prefer competition to access it while giving others options that better fit their learning preferences.

• **Help students focus on learning.** When students engage in a competitive activity (such as the examples above), emphasize the work students are doing over the winning and losing of the game. For example, after students have practiced "ea" words, instead of asking who won, you might ask students to share a couple of interesting words they found. As students play, especially if some seemed overly focused on the competition aspect of the activity, you can remind them: "Enjoy the game, and also remember the important skills you're practicing."

Teach Skills of Cooperation and Collaboration

One of the most important things you can do to help build a choice-ready learning environment—one where students will work with others in a variety of contexts—is to make sure kids have the skills they need to work well with each other. Especially with older students, it is easy to assume they already know how to work with others. "Cooperate!" we demand. "You should know how to get along in a group!" we admonish. In fact, we need to teach students the skills they need to be successful. This will vary depending on the needs of your students and the nature of the choice activity in which they are engaged. Figure 2.4 includes a few examples to spark your thinking:

2.4 A Few Cooperation and Collaboration Skills		
Context	**Skills Kids Might Need**	**Ideas for Supporting Them**
Some students have chosen to practice sight words with a partner. They will quiz each other using flash cards they have made.	Deciding who goes first	Ask the class for a few ideas and have partners pick one.
	Offering kind encouragement when someone is struggling	Model and offer phrases to use: ("Keep trying! You can do it!").
Students will work with a lab partner on a chemical change experiment they have chosen.	Deciding who will take responsibility for different parts of the lab	Have partners write out all responsibilities, estimate amount of work, and divide fairly.
	How to come to agreement if there are different opinions about what happened in the experiment	Brainstorm ideas as a class, leaving an anchor chart for pairs to refer to when needed.
Students will share pieces of writing with each other and offer feedback to help inform revisions.	Knowing how to give specific positive feedback and thoughtful suggestions	Practice as a class. Share a piece of your writing and have partners brainstorm positive comments and thoughtful suggestions they might give. Create a class chart of sentence starters for reference.

Though a worthy and important topic, it is well beyond the scope of this book to offer a complete approach for teaching social and emotional skills. Instead, here are a few ideas that might help guide you as you help students gain the skills needed for effective cooperation and collaboration.

• **Teach social and emotional skills.** It's not enough to demand of students, "Cooperate!" any more than it is enough to tell students, "Multiply!" They must be shown how to do this and have steps broken down.

• **Embed social and emotional skills instruction in academic lessons.** What skills will students need to practice to be successful with the work in front of them? Blend those skills in with the academic teaching. For example, to have an effective writing conference, students will need to make good eye contact. As you model a good writing conference, draw students' attention to the eye contact you use, and encourage them to practice that as they confer.

• **Give students time to practice.** Just like academic skills, social and emotional skills require repetition and practice. Many students will need a lot of time and multiple points of instruction to gain the skills needed.

For more information about social and emotional learning, check out CASEL (Collaborative for Academic, Social, and Emotional Learning): www.casel.org.

Conclusion

This chapter has explored many ways to build a classroom community that is safe, inclusive, and collaborative—all characteristics that will help students feel safe enough to make the best choices for their learning. It's important to note that while this kind of environment will certainly make choice more effective, the payoffs go well beyond times when students are engaged in choice. *Any* learning environment will benefit when a classroom environment is safe enough for students to take risks and inclusive enough so that all students feel like they belong and are respected.

CHAPTER 3

Boosting Student Ownership

A sense of student ownership of work is one of the most important qualities teachers should foster in their classrooms for students to be more successful with choice. When students make choices about their learning, they should focus on what *they* need and want. If students are hooked into pleasing the teachers or meeting the teachers' demands, they may not make choices that are either the right level of difficulty or the right modality. Also, when students do put themselves in a "just right" place of learning, there is appropriate challenge. This often means that students will need to work hard. When students' intrinsic motivation is higher—when they care about their work because the work is *theirs*—they will more likely have the determination needed to persevere when the learning gets tough.

This chapter will explore practical strategies for boosting student ownership of work so that they can better challenge themselves through choice.

Classroom Design

In Mr. Fortier's classroom, maps of the world, posters about Ancient Greece, a chart of the democratic process, and other content displays cover much of the walls. A faint outline around the posters hints at the number of years these posters have been in place. Students face the front of the room where Mr. Fortier's desk sits next to the interactive white board—a focus for many class lectures and discussions. On Mr. Fortier's desk and on the surrounding walls are pictures of his family, pennants of his favorite sports teams, and mementos of trips he has taken. Above the door of the classroom, a placard states the obvious: "Mr. Fortier's Room."

Next door in Ms. Fitzgerald's room, the feeling is quite different. The walls display current student work and anchor charts from recent lessons. Student seating is flexible, and students shift where they work depending on the work they are doing. Student cubbies and supply caddies keep materials and supplies organized so students can work anywhere easily. An instructional area is situated around the interactive white board, but the space is relatively small, indicating that direct instruction is concise—students spend more time doing than listening. "Team Adventure," a name chosen by the students at the beginning of the year, hangs above the classroom door.

Both rooms are friendly, warm, and safe environments, but the ownership of the room feels different. While students are in Mr. Fortier's classroom, Ms. Fitzgerald's students are in their own. This may affect how students feel about their work. When offered choices in Mr. Fortier's more teacher-centric classroom, students may be more likely to pick the ones they think he prefers, or they may feel a diminished sense of ownership of work in general. In Ms. Fitzgerald's class students may be more inclined to choose options based on their learning needs, because they are the primary focus of the classroom.

A colleague of mine mentioned that a friend of his teaches in Germany. In his school, the teachers rotate from classroom to classroom while students stay in one space all day. Just think about the powerful message that sends to students about who owns the space and the learning! While this may be too dramatic a shift for many educators, there are lots of ways you might boost students' sense of ownership through the classroom design.

• **Walls and display spaces.** A visitor to the classroom should be able to "read" the walls and know what work is happening and who is doing it. Hang current student work (both in process and finished work) around the room along with student names and even photos. (Especially in upper grades, it may be a good idea to ask students' permission before posting anything.) Take down charts or posters when they're not in use. Consider having student volunteers help post work and displays on the walls to increase student ownership while decreasing your workload.

• **Instructional areas.** In a classroom designed for choice most of students' time is spent working, not listening. However, there still needs to be a place for whole-group instruction or sharing. In younger-grade classrooms this may be on a rug or circle area. In upper-grade classrooms, students may move furniture into an arc or cluster desks and tables together as needed. Ideally, this space can easily be used for small-group instruction as well.

• **Teacher work space.** Some teachers decide to ditch their desk altogether and work at the same tables and desks as their students. If this isn't possible, you might consider reducing the size of your desk area to make more room for student work space. Push the desk against a wall or move it into a back corner. Also consider how many personal pictures and artifacts you keep in the room. A few can help students connect with you and help you feel at home while at school. Too many may send the message that the room is more yours than the students', when ideally, it should be shared and have a feeling of collective ownership.

• **Cultural considerations.** Think about your students' backgrounds and families. As they look around the room, do they see their cultures and values reflected in the space? Do posters, displays, books, and other resources reflect who they are? Are there displays in the room that might alienate or exclude some students? For example, Christmas displays might make non-Christian students feel like they're on the outside looking in. Instead, you might consider decorations that match the season (snowflakes) instead of the holiday (Christmas trees). In one school where I have worked, all of the students were Native American. Posters and artwork on the walls, themes of schoolwide assemblies, and even the color schemes of paint throughout the building all reflect the heritage of the students, helping them feel a greater sense of inclusion and personal connection to school.

Language That Boosts Ownership

Language sends important messages about who owns the work in the classroom, and through thoughtful consideration of what you say, and how you say it, you can help boost students' sense of ownership of learning.

Focusing on Students

One way to shift language to help convey the idea that the work belongs to the students is to talk in the second person instead of the first. When teachers talk in the first person, they are naturally the focus. When they shift to the second person, students are. Speaking in the second person encourages teachers to see the work through students' eyes and emphasize their role in the work (see Figure 3.1). Although certainly not appropriate all of the time, an interesting exercise is to pay attention to your language and see if there are times when using the "you" voice instead of the "I" voice might increase student ownership of work.

Rethinking Praise

While it is important to give students positive feedback, many researchers and authors over the past few decades have shed light on the dangers of traditional praise. Alfie Kohn asserts that praise diminishes intrinsic motivation (1993). Carol Dweck's research highlights how praising students' abilities can put students in a fixed mindset—one that can diminish their ability to learn (2006). Paula Denton argues that connecting praise with personal approval

3.1
Suggestions for Shifting Voice

Instead of . . .	Try . . .
"There are still some people in here who owe me homework from last night."	"Make sure to turn in your homework from last night."
"I'd love to see some great effort on this next project."	"Some great effort will help your work really shine in this next project."
"I'm going to give you three choices for how to learn about Pablo Picasso."	"You're going to have three choices for how to learn about Pablo Picasso."
"This quiz will help me figure out where you all are in your understanding of this unit so far."	"This quiz will help you figure out where you are in your understanding of this unit so far."
"Would someone raise your hand and show me what you have so far?"	"Would someone raise your hand and show what you have so far?"
"I want you to find a topic that is important to you."	"Think about a topic that is important to you."

("I love the way you worked so hard!") may hook students into working to please the teacher instead of focusing on work for their own sense of satisfaction (2014, p. 97). In a detailed analysis of research on praise, Hattie and Yates (2014) found that it has no positive impact on learning.

But if we shouldn't praise students, how can we offer them positive feedback in ways that increase their autonomy and intrinsic motivation—ways that will help reinforce the idea that they are the ones who ultimately own their work? A key strategy is to think about the values and messages behind our positive feedback. "I like the way you solved that math problem" may send the message to students that they should solve math problems in a certain way because you like it. Instead, we want them to value the work itself, so we might say, "You used several different strategies to solve that math problem. That shows strong math thinking." Figure 3.2 offers a few other examples.

3.2
Suggestions for Positive Feedback

Values to Promote	Instead of ...	Try ...
Intrinsic motivation is more important than teacher-pleasing.	"Wow! That is an amazing poem! I'm so proud of you!"	"Wow! That is an amazing poem! You must be so proud of your work!"
Hard work (not innate intelligence) is the key to success.	"You got that tough math problem right! You're so smart!"	"You just worked on that one math problem for a long time, and you got it!"
Self-reflection and self-assessment are important.	"Let me tell you what I think about your work."	"What are some qualities of your work that you are most pleased with?"
The good of the group is motivation for teamwork.	"I love the way you are working together as a team!"	"You're really working together as a team. That's helping you get some great work done!"
Students should listen to each other.	Student responds to a question: "I think Lincoln is the best president." Teacher echoes: "Lincoln!"	Student responds to a question: "I think Lincoln is the best president." Teacher: (Nods in recognition.)
Quality work, not compliance, should drive effort.	"To earn full credit for these problems, you have to show me your work."	"Show your work to illustrate how you thought through each problem."

Constructive Feedback

When students have chosen aspects of their work and are therefore invested in it, they are more receptive to constructive feedback. Quality now matters. And just like certain kinds of encouraging language might better foster a sense of ownership and intrinsic motivation, the way in which we offer constructive feedback can reinforce students' self-motivation, making them more likely to engage in choice in ways that are authentic and beneficial. After all, when students are self-motivated about their work, they're not just open to constructive feedback—they crave it.

The way in which we offer this feedback is important. It must be concrete and offer manageable suggestions—pushes that are within the grasp of students so that they can see that the effort needed to try them is worth taking. The feedback should also be concrete and clear, yet supportive and kind in tone; while we shouldn't sugarcoat suggestions, there's also no need to be harsh. Students feel valued when they get direct and caring feedback, but if we are unnecessarily critical or mean, they'll withdraw, shut down, and be unwilling to take the risks needed to choose appropriate learning tasks. Figure 3.3 includes a few examples.

3.3
Suggestions for Constructive Feedback

Context	Instead of . . .	Try . . .
To a sports team getting ready for a big game . . . (replace criticism with encouragement)	"That was horrible! We'll never advance in the playoffs if we keep playing like that!"	"That play still needs a lot of work. We're going to need to give that some extra work so we're ready for the playoffs."
In a conference about a piece of writing . . . (replace accusation with suggestion)	"Why haven't you added more detail to this piece? We spent a lot of time this week working on adding detail, and you haven't done it yet!"	"Think about some of the work we've done this week on how to add detail. As you look at your piece of writing, where are some places you think detail might help?"
With a small group that seems to be floundering with a task . . . (replace negative assumption with positive one)	"You guys are really fooling around and wasting time. Knock it off."	"It looks like your group is struggling. What can I do to help you get back on track?"
For a student who is upset about doing poorly on an assignment . . . (replace guilt with empathy)	"I'm so disappointed in you. You could have done much better."	"I know you're upset. Let's think together about what you can do to improve this."

Rethinking Incentives

Despite decades of research that highlight the ineffectiveness of incentives both in schools and in the workplace (Kohn, 1993; Pink, 2009), they are still surprisingly prevalent in schools. Students earn stickers, candy, and prizes for good work and behavior. Schools post names and pictures of "Star Citizens" or "Hard Worker Awards" in hallway displays. Award ceremonies highlight the accomplishments of a few at the end of the year. In all of these examples, it is clearly the adults who have the control and own the work, and the incentives are designed to get students to do something that is assumed they don't want to do already. Though they are well intentioned, these practices tend to demotivate students, damage relationships, and foster resentment and jealousy. One way to foster a classroom environment of mutual respect and collaboration is to eliminate rewards and incentive programs.

As researcher and professor of psychology Edward Deci so convincingly concludes in his important book *Why We Do What We Do* (1995), extrinsic rewards dampen intrinsic motivation and decrease performance. Students may be intrinsically motivated to accomplish a task—because it is challenging, interesting, or fun—but incentivizing student behavior through the offer of rewards saps this intrinsic drive. Students will tend to focus on the allure of the prize over the satisfaction of the work. Once students are offered a pizza party or cash for accomplishing something, when they aren't offered rewards in the next round, they quickly lose motivation. This dramatically decreases their ownership of the work, because the work is no longer the goal, the incentive is.

Just think of how confusing this kind of system might be for students engaged in choice. "It's your job to choose problems to solve that are appropriately challenging, and you'll get to pull a prize out of the treat bag for every 10 problems you answer correctly!" If you were a student and heard that message, what would you choose, problems that were appropriately challenging or ones that you could solve accurately and quickly?

Celebrations Instead of Rewards

Does this mean we should never recognize students' hard work or behavior? No! In fact, celebrating hard work and a job done well can have a positive effect on the climate and culture of a classroom, allowing students to bask in

3.4	
Incentive vs. Celebration	
Instead of . . .	**Try . . .**
(On Monday) We've got a lot of work to do in order to be ready to publish our fairy tales in our class anthology. If you work really hard and get a lot done, we'll watch a great fairy tale movie, *The Princess Bride*, as a reward.	(On Friday) Phew! We've put in a lot of hard work this week and accomplished a lot. We're ready to put together our class anthology! Let's celebrate! We're going to watch one of the great fairy tales of all time: *The Princess Bride*!

collective success while building more positive feelings about work and learning. The key is to celebrate without incentivizing. Consider the different messages the two scenes in Figure 3.4 send.

In the first scene, students may be eager to watch a movie, but the message sent is that the teacher believes they don't want to work hard and need to be bribed to do so. This will make the writing feel more like work, decreasing intrinsic drive and shifting motivation from doing great writing for the anthology to trying to earn a movie at the end of the week. Students may feel manipulated. Students who don't work hard may be pressured by others to do so, diminishing a sense of positive community in the room. In the second scene, the feeling is celebratory. Students feel good about their accomplishments and are excited to celebrate together with a fun movie.

Here are a few other ways you can make sure that celebrations build intrinsic motivation, boost ownership, and foster a positive sense of community.

• **Celebrate collectively.** Whether through simple positive feedback ("Congratulations, everyone! That science lab was challenging, and as a class, we persisted and gathered some really interesting data!") or a more formal celebration, such as an end-of-unit event, focus on the accomplishments of the group over individual successes. This will boost a positive sense of belonging and academic success.

• **Avoid if-then statements.** "If you work really hard for the next 30 minutes then you can have some free time at the end of the period!" is an incentivizing statement—a bribe—that will decrease intrinsic motivation and ownership. Instead, allow celebrations to be spontaneous.

• **Recognize all learners.** A class display in the hallway that showcases student poetry should include every student in the class, not just the ones deemed most accomplished.

Purposeful Work

"Mr. Anderson, why do we have to do this?" is one of my favorite questions to get from a student. It highlights a positive need on the part of students to see purpose in their work. In order to really own the work, students need to know why they are doing it or why it is important.

It can be easy to get so caught up in the *what* students are doing that it's easy for teachers to forget to explain the *why*. Importantly, the why explanation needs to resonate with learners, so give the explanation from a perspective that matters to them (see Figure 3.5). "It's part of the curriculum" or "It's on the upcoming standardized test" likely won't inspire a lot of student investment. Instead, connect with students' goals, tap into their interests, ideas,

3.5 Examples of Purposeful Work	
Grade 1, Science: Waves, Light, and Sound Plan and conduct investigations to determine the effect of placing objects made with different materials in the path of a beam of light.	**Tap into Natural Curiosity** "Have you ever noticed that different kinds of materials affect light differently? Some let light pass through, some let a little bit of light through, some block light, and some reflect it. You're going to get to choose a whole bunch of different materials to explore today to check that out!"
Grade 5, Reading: Analyzing Fiction Critically During a genre study of fantasy and science fiction writing, students will choose a text to explore and examine critically.	**Reinforce Benefit** "You can get so much more out of a book if you read it critically. During our next genre study, you're going to get to choose a book in the fantasy or science fiction genre and read it closely, examining characters, exploring themes, and considering how authors were inspired."
Grade 8, Writing: Research Citations "Quote or paraphrase the data and conclusions of others while avoiding plagiarism and following a standard format for citation" (CCSS. ELA-Literacy.W.8.8).	**Place in the Context of More Purposeful Work** "Citing sources can sometimes feel tedious, but it's a really important part of your research projects. It gives credit where credit is due and helps your research be both more legitimate and legal."
Grade 11: Geometry Students will apply sine and cosine functions to real-world problems.	**Connect to Real-World Learning** "Professionals in many fields use sine and cosine functions to solve problems. Today, you're going to choose one that interests you. You can work on one involving tides, Ferris wheels, or surveying."

and natural curiosity, and help them see how the work they are engaged in is important for them. It is also important to anticipate and pre-think the "why are we doing this" question. Sometimes we are teaching something because it's mandated or simply part of the curriculum, and we may need to figure out a student-resonant explanation in case the question arises!

Another way to help build student ownership of work—and one that can have important, direct connections to choice—is to have students engage in meaningful goal-setting. At the beginning of the year or at the start of a new semester, you might have students write down a few academic goals. This can also work well at the beginning of a new unit of study. What do they hope to learn? What skills do they hope to improve? Encourage students to share goals that are meaningful and directly connected with upcoming work. This helps them create personal relevance for the work at hand while helping you consider meaningful choices you might offer—ones that will directly connect with students' goals.

Assessment and Grading

In a fascinating study, Edward Deci and a graduate student had two groups of college students work at learning complex neurophysiology content. Half of the students were told they would be tested and graded on their learning while the other half were told they would learn the material to teach it to others. Not only were students who were told they would be tested and graded less motivated (as measured by a questionnaire), but they actually learned less than the ones who were learning to teach others—especially interesting because the second group had not been told they would be tested (1995, p. 47).

This has an important consequence in classrooms where students will have choices about their learning. When grades are designed to motivate students, their attention is focused on what hoops to jump through to get a grade instead of on what they need to do to learn. This will then weigh heavily on their decision-making process when making choices: "Should I choose something easy? Will that mean I get more right answers and a better grade? Or should I choose something really challenging, because that will impress the teacher, leading to a better grade?" This kind of thinking may lead students to choose work outside of their zone of proximal development, leading to a drop in engagement and learning.

Grade Less

For teachers who don't use grades, the idea of students being unmotivated unless they receive grades is a foreign concept. Each day, they see students working hard and doing great work without grades. For teachers who rely on grades to motivate, their worry that kids will stop trying if grades are removed is a valid one. Once students have been trained to view grades as the reason for doing work, it can be hard to break that. Their intrinsic drive has been replaced by an extrinsic one, and it takes work to undo the damage.

Additionally, urging teachers to simply stop grading is likely naïve and overly simplistic in many settings. Although some schools are moving away from traditional grading practices toward ones that focus on standards and competencies, many schools continue to require grading. So, consider deemphasizing grading, and grade less often. Especially when students are engaged in the learning of new content and the practicing of skills—times when you want students to own their work—they shouldn't be worried about being graded. Don't grade daily classwork, homework, and quizzes designed to see what students have mastered so far and what they still need to learn. Instead, offer simple verbal feedback, quick notes, or other forms of appropriate feedback.

Personalize Grading

Another way to help diminish the negative impacts of grading on choice is to personalize it for each student, especially when assessing complex work. That way, instead of all students having to be graded with the same criteria (a serious challenge if each student isn't doing the same thing), they are graded according to the particulars of the work they are doing. To even further boost students' ownership of work, have them help you with the process.

For example, a class of students has been learning about world religions. All students have crafted their own research projects in which they chose a religion to study, asked questions they wanted to answer (within required curricular themes), and developed a few projects to share their learning with others. Students have a checklist to help them keep track of required content as well as their own goals. They fill in their own project details so that as the teacher grades their work, the checklists have been personalized (see Figure 3.6). If you don't need to use grades, this same checklist could be used without the point system. Teachers simply check off boxes as students accomplish learning objectives.

3.6 World Religion Research and Project Guide	
Name: *Macy* **Religion:** *Taoism*	
Questions about History (10 pts.)	
When did Taoism start? *Who started it?* *Where did it first begin?*	_____ pts.
Questions about Beliefs (10 pts.)	
What are the most important beliefs in Taoism? *How did those beliefs start?* *Is there a book (like the Bible) that tells the beliefs?*	_____ pts.
Questions about Practices (10 pts.)	
What do Taoists do? *What's it like to be a kid in Taoism?* *Are there holidays? What are they?*	_____ pts.
Projects to Share (20 pts.)	
Timeline (history) *Prezi (beliefs and practices)* *Picture book (beliefs and practices)*	_____ pts.
Comments	

Use Grading Practices That Increase Responsibility

If you must use grades, consider practices that help students take more responsibility for their learning. For example, allowing students to retake a test, rewrite an essay, or re-present a project all send the same message: Grades reflect learning, and if you want a better grade, put in some more work and learn more. This can have a profound influence on how students view learning. Instead of a grade being a static letter or number—something that is supposed to reflect their intelligence—the grade is now a reflection of current progress. Knowing that they will have the opportunity to continue to work and learn may also help some students feel more comfortable making choices that are appropriately challenging.

Help Students Practice Self-Assessment

An important part of shifting ownership of learning is to help students develop skills of self-assessment. This tends to be much harder than it first appears, especially when students have been raised in systems that teach them to look to adults for judgment about their work and behavior. Simple practices such as rating yourself on a "fist-to-five" scale or having students show how they think something went with a "thumbs up," "thumbs down," or "thumbs to the side" are good places to start. More complex plans, like student-created rubrics and scoring sheets, can help students develop their self-assessment skills. The scoring guide shown in Figure 3.6 has been tweaked here in Figure 3.7 to show how a simple shift can help students self-assess. These scoring guides can then be great ways to start conversations with students about work. As you hear why students scored themselves in certain ways, you gain valuable insights into their self-reflection. You can then guide and coach them in ways that will help them grow.

Conclusion

I remember working at a job where a shift in ownership of the work profoundly affected my professional energy. When I first joined this workplace, there was a shared sense of ownership and autonomy. I had some real power and control

3.7 World Religion Research and Project Guide		
Name: Macy	**Religion:** Taoism	
Questions about History (10 pts.)	**Student Score**	**Teacher Score**
When did Taoism start? Who started it? Where did it first begin?	_____ pts.	_____ pts.
Questions about Beliefs (10 pts.)		
What are the most important beliefs in Taoism? How did those beliefs start? Is there a book (like the Bible) that tells the beliefs?	_____ pts.	_____ pts.
Questions about Practices (10 pts.)		
What do Taoists do? What's it like to be a kid in Taoism? Are there holidays? What are they?	_____ pts.	_____ pts.
Projects to Share (20 pts.)		
Timeline (history) Prezi (beliefs and practices) Picture book (beliefs and practices)	_____ pts.	_____ pts.
Comments		

over the kind of work that I did as well as the way in which I accomplished the work. Pouring my heart and soul into the work was easy. This shifted over time. Autonomy decreased, and more and more often, I was simply told what to do. When I was working, I no longer felt empowered to make judgments about the work—too often, someone else would come along and change what I had done, or the goals of the work would shift, requiring me to rework much of what I had already accomplished. I found myself feeling a bit like a worker bee—constantly busy, but in the service of someone else's goals. It became harder and harder to muster positive energy for the work, and eventually I decided that it was time to move on.

Similarly, students need to own their learning in order to be really successful with choice. That tone is set by you and needs to be done so thoughtfully and intentionally. It is one of the important ways that you can help boost the effectiveness of choice so that students can truly challenge themselves with their work.

CHAPTER 4

Teaching Students How to Learn

One of the most fundamental ideas behind student choice is that we are empowering students to make decisions about their own learning. But what if they don't know how to do this well?

As a child, I had no idea how learning worked. In elementary school, I did what teachers told me to do and somehow learned what I was supposed to learn. It was easy, and I felt good at school. As I got older, things changed in some ways and remained unchanged in others. In middle school, work was less fun, there was more of it, and I liked it less. I did the least amount possible and continued to be fairly successful—getting decent grades with little effort. I still felt smart.

In high school, I continued to work my way through school, sitting in class, doing activities, and completing assignments. However, as content became more complex, I didn't have the skill set needed to keep up. Stuck in what Carol Dweck would later coin as a fixed mindset (a topic we'll explore later in this chapter), I believed that if I was smart, I should just know what I was supposed to know. Or I should read something, hear a teacher say something, or try something once and "get it." Good grades no longer came so easily, and I learned very little. I also began to question my belief in my intelligence. Because school was no longer easy, I had a sneaking suspicion that I wasn't as smart as I had previously thought. Worried that others might catch on, I hid my struggles, rarely asked for help, and managed to squeak by.

It wasn't until I got to college that I actually began to learn how to learn. I suddenly realized that getting a good grade on a test required more than looking back over my notes, but that I actually had to write things down in multiple ways in order to remember them. Writing a good paper required me to write a crummy first draft, print it, mark it up, revise it multiple times, get meaningful feedback from professors or peers, and revise it some more. It helped that I was now surrounded by others who worked hard, studied together, and were genuinely interested in learning—a revelation to me. I now wonder what my education might have been like if I had learned how to learn before I was almost 20 years old.

This chapter will explore several ways you might teach students about learning and therefore empower them to be thoughtful, intentional, and self-reflective about their learning so they can make good choices. Like athletes who must understand how their bodies work—how muscle is built, the importance of stretching to prevent injury, the need for proper rest, food, and hydration— learners must understand how their minds work in order to use them effectively for learning.

Building Skills of Metacognition

I'm sure you've heard the old adage: "Give a man a fish, and he'll eat for a day. Teach a man to fish, and he'll eat forever." Teaching skills of metacognition is the educational equivalent of teaching students to fish. We're helping them develop skills of self-awareness, self-reflection, and honest self-assessment needed to become life-long learners. And yet, given the frenetic pace of schooling today, it's easy to move from one activity to the next, keeping students busy—focused on *what* they are doing, without helping them reflect on *how* they are learning. This becomes increasingly relevant as you share power and control of learning with students through offering choice. Students need the chance to build their metacognitive skill set—or, as neurologist and teacher Judy Willis says, to make "the unconscious conscious" (2006, p. 33).

Like all other skills, metacognition is something that can be taught, practiced, and developed. You can help your students know themselves as learners, keep track of learning strategies that are personally helpful, and act in ways that use this self-knowledge to improve their learning. Of course, choice, especially when used with the choose-do-review framework (explained in Chapters 6, 7, and 8), can be a great vehicle for boosting skills of metacognition. Both the "choose" and "review" stages are particularly well suited to helping students practice metacognition. That being said, in order to get the most out of these steps, there are other ways you can teach and support your learners' metacognitive skills.

Demonstrate Metacognition

One way to help students learn skills of metacognition is to demonstrate your own thinking, sharing personal examples of ways you use your self-knowledge to boost your learning. For example, a high school teacher who is helping students prepare for a test might offer the following self-reflection: "I know that some find that studying in a group is most effective. As much as I love being with other people, the best way for me to study is alone. When I'm with others, I tend to get off track. When I'm alone, I can review notes, write information in several ways, and quiz myself, and those all help me remember key ideas."

You can also model what it looks and sounds like to think something through. This is especially helpful for students who need to see something in action. For example, you might model choosing a new book: "I love fantasy books, so I think I might try *Eragon*. On the other hand, I sometimes lose interest in really long books, so I'm not sure this is a great choice. Maybe I'll try the first few chapters and see how it goes." You could also use this "think-aloud" strategy to show how to use a particular strategy to struggle through a tough math problem. "Argh! I get frustrated with really long word problems. I'm going to use a highlighter to mark the key words. Maybe that will help me focus on what I need to pay attention to."

Use Open-Ended Questions to Prompt Reflective Thinking

As Paula Denton writes in *The Power of Our Words*, "open-ended questions are those for which there is no single right or wrong answer" (2014, p. 47). They are powerful tools for building students' powers of self-reflection because they "draw on students' own thoughts, knowledge, skills, experiences, and feelings"

(2014, p. 47). Use open-ended questions throughout the learning process to help students develop and practice metacognition:

• **While choosing.** "What are some key characteristics you look for in a good book?" "Think about yourself as a learner—what are some things you could use practice with during today's workshop time?" "What might it look like and feel like if you created problems that were at your just right level?"

• **While doing.** "What is working well for you right now as a learner?" "What should you keep doing and what might you adjust?" "What do you think your next steps might be?"

• **While reviewing.** "Think back over the work time. What learning strategies worked for you? Which ones might you try next time?" "If you had these same three choices tomorrow, would you choose the same way you did today? Why?"

An Idea to Try: A Self-Reflection Journal

Students can keep a simple journal to help them reflect on their learning. The body of the journal can be used as a space for students to write about their learning on a daily basis, answering open-ended questions posed by the teacher or reflecting in general on their learning. In the back of the journal, students can keep track of strategies that are especially effective (see Figure 4.1).

4.1	
Sample Self-Reflection Journal	
Daily Reflections	**Strategies That Help Me Learn**
(2/12/15) Today during our science lab, I chose to work on my own. A positive was that I got a lot done and was efficient with time. On the downside, I wish I'd had someone to work with. When I got confused I had to keep bothering other people—a lab partner would have been nice. *(2/17/15) We have a test coming up. I'm going to invite Lisa and Charmaine over for a study group. Having others to talk through ideas with will help me understand them.*	*• Rereading: Skimming a text first and then reading more deeply helps me understand.* *• Drawing pictures: Sketching a science process forces me to think visually and helps me put things into words.* *• Highlighting: When I highlight key ideas in a text, I remember them. I also know what questions to ask.* *• Mnemonics: When I create an acronym for something, I remember it better.*

Periodically have students review their journal to reflect on what they have recorded, helping to strengthen and deepen their skills of self-reflection.

An Idea to Try: A Self-Knowledge Self-Portrait

Have students draw full-body self-portraits and keep them in a place where students can return to them over and over—perhaps by hanging them on a bulletin board or keeping them in a folder in their desk or cubby. Have students annotate the portraits with notes about their learning. A note near an ear might say, "I learn well by listening" and a sticky note by a hand might say, "I like to use my hands." Several self-portraits, created throughout the year, will paint an interesting picture of students' developing self-awareness.

Teaching Honest Self-Assessment

As a classroom teacher, I have seen many students struggle with being able to accurately self-assess their work and progress. Often, students who are strong and competent are overly self-critical, underestimating their work or abilities, while students who struggle or underperform tend to be too generous in their self-assessment, either not seeing or glossing over areas of weakness. Interestingly, this experience reflects a study where researchers asked university students to estimate their scores after taking an exam. When their scores were analyzed and compared to their self-assessments, the top 25 percent scored better than they thought, and the bottom 25 percent overestimated their scores by an average of 20 points. This study is just one of many that reflects the challenges people have in accurate self-assessment (Hattie & Yates 2014, pp. 233–234).

This is important for this discussion of choice because in order to maximize the value of choice, students must self-assess well so they can place themselves in the zone of proximal development where they learn best. It will also help them be better at goal-setting and revision, both important skills that help drive more meaningful self-directed work. Here are a few suggestions for helping build students' skills of self-reflection:

• **Practice daily.** Students might use a "thumbs up, thumbs down" or "fist-to-five" reflection to rate how well a work period went. These quick and simple self-assessments give students lots of practice in the skills of self-assessing in settings where it is safe to be honest.

• **Help make self-assessments concrete.** As students reflect on their work, have them name specific attributes of their work to back up their self-assessments. Prompts such as "Name one aspect of your work that was strong today" and "What is one thing that could have been better?" can help students be more specific and thoughtful as they self-assess.

• **Coach students individually.** As you confer with students and see them struggling with accurate self-assessment, give them kind and clear feedback. "Juan, I hear you saying that you think this short story isn't very good. You have a strong opening, an interesting story line, and well-developed characters. You are including all of the elements of short story narratives that we're working on." Or "Linda, I know that you think this PowerPoint presentation is ready to go, but it still needs some work. There are several misspelled words, and a few of the slides have too much text."

Be Patient and Persistent

Like any skill, metacognition requires time, practice, and guidance to develop. Use simple strategies and weave language and activities into daily academic work that help students learn how to think about their own thinking. Over time, with many opportunities to reflect and think about their learning, and with your ongoing guidance and patience, students will become more skilled at reading themselves and using that self-knowledge to make choices that will best help them learn.

Teach About the Zone of Proximal Development

In order for students to make choices that are appropriately challenging (a very specific metacognitive skillset), they need to know just what that means. The terminology you use and the way in which you teach this to students will depend on their developmental level. Young children might best connect with the idea through the story of Goldilocks and the Three Bears, or they might best understand the terminology of a "just right" zone. Older students might appreciate the advanced sounding language of the "zone of proximal development" with a bit of background about Lev Vygotsky. Regardless of the language you use, all learners need to understand and connect with the notion that learning is at its peak and is most enjoyable in this zone.

The idea of challenge being enjoyable may seem foreign to some students, especially ones who have experienced education as a long series of uninspiring tasks handed to them by someone else. Interestingly, most students who struggle with academic grit often display incredible tenacity in other areas of their lives. You can help students connect personally and positively with this idea of appropriate challenge by helping them see themselves as hard working and motivated, and connecting those attributes to their success in those other areas.

- **Sports.** Have students think about skills they have developed in sports. Chances are, they develop those skills through hard work in the zone of proximal development. You might also ask them which games are the most exciting and fun, ones where the score is a blowout or ones where both teams are evenly matched—where each team pushes each other to the limit.

- **Video games.** If a game is too easy and requires no effort or challenge, players quickly bore and disconnect. When the game is impossibly hard and players can't win and see no possibility of doing so, they become overly frustrated and disconnect. Games in which players master levels and then move onto the next challenge are appealing precisely because they continuously position players in the zone of proximal development.

- **The arts.** A student might spend hours and hours dancing, singing, or playing an instrument, which has led to a high skill set. Students may draw race cars, faces, or comics over and over again, crafting their drawings with a critical eye. Help them see all of that effort, which they would likely call "fun" or "play," as enjoyable hard work.

Of course, there are many other skills that students may have acquired through practice and effort: cooking, skateboarding, computer programing, and many more. By using these personal examples to highlight what it means to practice something in the zone of proximal development, you can help students transfer this skill set and attitude to academic learning.

Another idea to consider is that the "just right" zone will be different depending on the particular goals of the activity. If students are working on complex multi-step word problems in class, you might encourage students to find a "just right" zone that is near the edge of their frustration level because peers and teachers are on hand to coach and support. On the other hand, if students are practicing analyzing character development in novels, they should choose books that they can read independently. The reading itself should be relatively easy, otherwise their fluency will break down and they won't be able to practice the reading analysis skills. Similarly, students who have a leveled choice as a part of a homework assignment should choose something they can do independently, because they will be working on their own with little, if any, support and at a time of day when they are already tired. What is important about this idea in general is that you need to help students learn how to realistically match the level of difficulty of the work they are choosing to the expectations and setting of the work.

Teaching and Promoting a Growth Mindset

Carol Dweck and her research team at Stanford University have conducted numerous studies that show that people's belief in their own ability to learn has a profound impact on their achievement. One who has a *fixed mindset* believes that he or she is smart or not, has a skill or doesn't, and that there's little to do about either. Someone with a *growth mindset* understands that hard work and effort lead to growth, learning, and competence. Dweck has also shown that people can be put into a fixed or growth mindset in a given situation. Seemingly simple statements such as "You're so smart!" can lead students to land in a fixed mindset, diminishing their effort and effectively closing their minds to growth as they work to protect an image of intelligence-by-gift (Dweck, 2006).

Helping students develop a growth mindset may be one of the most important things educators do in a learning environment in which students will challenge themselves through choice, because appropriate self-differentiation requires that students value effort and challenge—to be more concerned with growing and learning than with getting answers correct or finishing quickly. Dweck and her team uncovered that students in a growth mindset tend to relish challenging tasks, seeing them as an opportunity for learning, while students in a fixed mindset shied away from challenges, not wanting to expose their flaws (2006, p. 72). I have seen this work in the reverse direction as well; students choose options that are way too difficult, believing that looking smart is more important that learning.

There are many ways you might help your students develop growth mindsets, so let's explore a few.

Teacher as Model: Demonstrating a Growth Mindset

Our students watch us more than you might imagine, and the ways in which we speak about our own growth and learning—the mindsets we model—set the tone for our students. This means we need to be aware of, and intentional about, the mindsets we demonstrate on a daily basis.

This may be especially hard if we, as teachers, haven't yet developed a growth mindset. I know that many times, I have accidentally modeled a fixed mindset for my students. "I'm terrible at drawing," I said when sketching a diagram in science class. "I've never been good at remembering dates," I admitted while looking something up during a history lesson. When I realized the effect statements like these were having on my students, I made a conscious effort to speak about my own abilities in ways that reflected the kinds of attitudes I wanted my students to have about theirs.

Perhaps in an effort to appear modest, to make a risk feel less risky, or to make students feel good, teachers may speak about themselves in self-deprecating ways, engage in negative self-talk, or diminish their own talents intentionally. Whether they do so out of a genuine fixed mindset or with the intention of boosting students' egos, it's a professional habit that teachers should collectively break. Even if you don't yet *have* a growth mindset, you can still *demonstrate* one through your language and actions (see Figure 4.2).

Teacher as Mirror: Language That Supports Growth

Similarly, the language teachers use to reflect students' learning can help set either a fixed or growth mindset in students. When teachers praise students' abilities ("You're so smart!" "You are such a great musician!"), students

4.2
Language: Teachers as Learners

Scene	Fixed Mindset	Growth Mindset
Sharing a piece of personal writing to demonstrate a skill or technique in a middle school writing lesson	"I'm not a very good writer, but let me show you one way to describe a character."	"This is still a rough draft, and I have some revising to do. Let me show you how I'm working at describing a character."
Talking with high school students between classes about an upcoming band concert	"I've never been good at music. I played the clarinet in high school and was terrible!"	"I wish I'd worked harder at music as a kid. I played the clarinet in high school, but I didn't put in the practice time needed to make the marching band."
During a read aloud, a 1st grader exclaims: "You're a great reader!"	"I love to read. It's always something I've been good at."	"I love to read. I've practiced a lot, ever since I was a kid!"

may take on less challenging tasks or stop asking questions, focusing instead on maintaining the appearance of intelligence (Dweck, 2007). So, as you celebrate students' achievements, coach them toward success, and help them get back on track when needed, use language that fosters the belief that hard work and effort, not talent, is the key to success. Help them see themselves as learners (see Figure 4.3).

4.3
Language: Students as Learners

Scene	Fixed Mindset	Growth Mindset
A class had a rough day with a substitute teacher the day before.	"I guess this is the kind of class that can't be trusted when I'm not around!"	"Let's think about some strategies you can use as a class the next time I need to be out of the room. I know you can do better than yesterday."
A student has crafted a poem that is stunningly good.	"This poem is amazing! You are such a talented writer."	"This poem has such depth of feeling with so few words! Tell me about how you wrote this!"
Classmates are talking about a student in the school who has just won a state level chess tournament.	"Chris is really talented, isn't he? It's like he was born holding a chess piece!"	"I bet Chris works really hard. How many hours a week do you think he plays chess to be that good?"

Teaching About Mindsets

Because students' mindsets are so crucial to their learning, let's teach them what a growth mindset is all about and why it is so important. There are many different ways to do this.

You could find an article or video that explains growth mindsets to students in age-appropriate ways, and have students explore the resource, offering them the choice of reflective questions to answer to prepare for a class discussion. You might have students name something they are good at (sports, video games, reading, fishing, etc.), and then have them name the strategies they used to get good at that skill (practice, hard work, effort, etc.). Then help them make the transfer. "You play soccer six days a week, and that has helped you become a solid player. The same will be true for reading. It takes practice and repetition."

You could also celebrate struggles. Promote the idea that failure is a pathway to success. People who never fail never learn. Have students share examples of times they have failed. Share some of your own failures. Create a wall display of rough drafts of work, complete with cross-outs, rewrites, and markups. Similarly, you can share stories of successful people with whom students can relate to illustrate the importance of hard work and growth. Of course, there are numerous examples, but here are a few to get the ball rolling: The Beatles, Michael Jordan, Bill Gates, Walt Disney, Thomas Edison, Oprah Winfrey, and Dr. Seuss.

As students learn to view hard work, effort, and true engagement as a pathway to learning—as they begin to develop a mindset that celebrates struggle and growth—they will be more likely to place themselves in the zone of proximal development or more likely to choose to take on learning that is centered around their needs and challenges.

Teaching About the Brain

One of Carol Dweck's recommendations for helping students develop a growth mindset involves teaching students how their brains work (2006, pp. 218–224). Through helping students understand the way neural pathways grow, the way information is shifted from working memory to long-term memory, the way excessive stress blocks memory storage and reasoning parts of the brain, and other such information about the brain, you can help students better understand how their minds work so they can take more control of their learning.

You can also talk about the brain in concrete and tangible ways. Statements like "You're going to need your brains for this next puzzle" and "You'll really be making your brains stronger through this next challenge" could help students remember the connection between struggle and intelligence, boosting their growth mindsets and setting them up to make better choices about their learning.

If you're interested in learning more about how the brain works and how that translates to effective teaching practices, I highly recommend *Research-Based Strategies to Ignite Student Learning* by Judy Willis (2006).

Conclusion

This is a good time to reflect for a moment, again, on why teaching students about learning is so important. Remember that when teachers hand over more power and control to students—as we give them more choices about their learning—we must also give them the skills and strategies to make good decisions. To ask students to make good choices without teaching them how to do so would be like handing a teenager the keys to a car without teaching him how to drive.

And, just as is the case with building safe and supportive learning environments and helping students take more ownership of their learning (which were discussed in the previous two chapters), it's important to recognize that one of the best ways to teach good decision making and help students learn to be better learners is through offering them choice. So again, these ideas go hand in hand and have a circular relationship rather than a linear one. If we decide we must first teach students all of the skills required to be self-reflective learners *before* offering choice, we'll never get there. Therefore we must teach skills of metacognition, explain the zone of proximal development, and promote growth mindsets *while* using choice.

This is where we're headed next. Now that we have explored some of the conditions needed to make it most effective, it's time to dig into the wonderful messiness of facilitating choice well.

THE NUTS AND BOLTS OF CHOICE

Now, in this final section of the book, it's time to roll up our sleeves and think about how to actually facilitate choice well. For although there is a wide variety of kinds of choice, many of which are quite simple (e.g., choosing between two worksheets; choosing to either work alone or with a partner), there's no getting around the fact that using choice with students makes things more complex. Of course, it's always nearly worth it, but only if it's done well, for choices that aren't matched to students' needs, or choices that get out of control and veer away from learning goals, won't have the benefits you're seeking.

Section III will help you explore the three-part process teachers should use to implement choice, which also includes the three-part process students should experience as a part of a complete choice experience.

Student Process

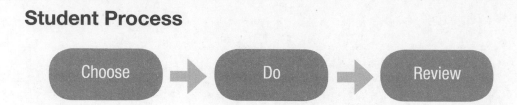

There are typically three stages of any good learning experience. Learners first think ahead about the work they are about to do, then they do the work, and then they think back about the work they just did. This tried and true "before-during-after" structure is a simple and effective process. A familiar example of this can be found in the reading and writing workshop approach to literacy instruction. Typically, each class begins with a mini-lesson that helps orient students to the skills and objectives of the day and provides some clear and concise direct instruction. Next, students read, write, confer, meet in a group, or engage in other rich literacy experiences. The period wraps up with a time for sharing and reflecting to help students consolidate learning.

A six-week unit in which groups of students study different topics and create different projects will involve much more time choosing than will a simple two-choice practice session involving vocabulary words. However, this basic structure will offer a starting place for your plans, regardless of whether you are using choice during a homework assignment, to structure learning on a field trip, to help students practice a skill, or to assess student learning at the end of a unit. There are a wide variety of terms used for this class three-part plan. Two common sets are opening-body-closing and initiation-work period-consolidation. In this book I use the terminology of choose-do-review, and each stage is discussed in-depth in Chapters 6–8.

Choose

During this first stage, teachers set students up to make good choices. They explain what the choices are so students can make informed decisions. Teachers provide both time and structures to help students make thoughtful choices.

Do

Once students have made their choice, they follow through and engage in the work at hand. Teachers serve as coaches, helping students as needed— guiding, supporting, troubleshooting, and encouraging—so students can be successful with their learning.

Review

Teachers provide students the chance to think back about what they learned, how they worked, and how their choice supported (or didn't support) their learning. This both helps drive home the learning and helps students develop skills of self-reflection that enable them to become more skilled at making effective choices in the future.

Teacher Process

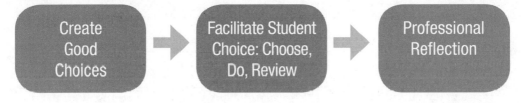

Just as there is a three-part structure you use to plan choice for students, so too, there is a three-part process in which you engage as a teacher planning and implementing choice. Chapter 5 will help you think about the first step of the teacher process, how to create choices that are meaningful for students— ones that directly connect with learning goals as well as students' needs and preferences. In Chapters 6, 7, and 8, you will learn how to facilitate choice well for students. You'll explore how to help students make good choices, support them as they work, and finally, help them review their choices and learning to deepen their abilities of self-reflection and effective decision making. Chapter 9 is a brief chapter that will help you complete the teacher planning process—reflecting on the choice experience so that you can grow in your implementation of choice.

CHAPTER 5

Creating Good Choices

Create Good Choices	→	Facilitate Student Choice: Choose, Do, Review	→	Professional Reflection

Christine stands in front of the class, her eyes beaming with pride. Students in my 4th grade class have spent the last week creating projects to share what they have learned about the solar system. Christine has studied the sun. She has collected many interesting facts, organized them into categories, and worked hard on her project, and she is excited to share it with the class. I have been impressed with her efforts, for Christine is a student who sometimes struggles with following through on a plan and often doesn't put a lot of energy into schoolwork. This project, however, is different. She has been so enthusiastic about the idea of painting a giant sun costume and has poured so much time and effort into her work, meticulously constructing a sun (no small feat for 4th grade fingers that tire quickly using scissors to cut through rigid cardboard) and then painting every square inch of it in various shades of yellow and orange, that neither of us has considered whether or not a giant sun costume is a good choice for her content.

Christine's presentation falls flat. She is justifiably proud of her sun costume, but she doesn't have much to say. She stammers through an explanation of her costume and how hard she has worked on it, looks nervously down at her notes and shares some of the facts she had learned, takes a few questions from her classmates, and sits back down.

I'm not sure that Christine fully understood what happened that day, but I learned a valuable lesson: Choice as a strategy is only effective if the choices themselves are good ones. That is the focus of this chapter—creating good choices. After all, although choice is an amazing strategy that can fit many different situations in any grade or content area, here's another important time to remember that choice is a means to an end, not an end in and of itself. Choice should only be used if it will enhance student learning, either by helping students engage in work that is appropriately challenging or by boosting motivation by tapping into strengths, interests, or needs. A teacher I once worked with aptly stated: "Four bad choices are worse than none at all." Poor choices can discourage learners, waste time, and dampen enthusiasm for learning. There are many times when choice is not an appropriate strategy, so do not force it when it's not a good fit. When it is a good fit, make sure to create options that will enhance student learning.

So, what exactly are *good* choices? How do you know whether options are good ones or not? Especially if using choice as a strategy in daily learning is something new, it can feel overwhelming. Where do you start? This chapter covers the key characteristics of choices that will enhance learning. Through considering each of these characteristics, teachers can create options for students that will make the highest potential impact on their work.

Choices Should Match Learning Goals

Christine's sun project wasn't a good fit because painting a giant cardboard cutout of the sun did nothing to reinforce or help share content she was supposed to learn. She was highly engaged, but the engagement wasn't connected with the learning goals, so it didn't pay any real dividends on learning science content. This is perhaps the most important characteristic of good choices—they must match students' learning goals. Consider the two following sources for student goals: (1) standards, content, and curricula and (2) process goals.

Standards, Content, Curricula

When thinking of possible choices for students, begin with the academic content goals. What are students supposed to be learning? If you're not crystal clear about this, your choices may not end up being a good fit. For example, as a first-year teacher, I remember asking a colleague what our first science unit was. "Prairie dogs," she answered. "Prairie dogs? Why prairie dogs?" I remember replying. As it turns out, the first chapter in the science textbook was all about prairie dogs—as a way of helping students learn about animals that live in communities. Though prairie dogs may be cute, I wasn't sure this topic was going to resonate with all of my students. Once I understood the true goal of the science unit, I was able to structure choices that gave students more control over some of the content (which animals to study) while meeting the important learning goals of the unit (understanding the characteristics of animals that live in communities). Small teams of students chose animals they were interested in that lived in communities, and each team had to learn the key content outlined in the science text (different roles in the group, social hierarchy, etc.). Students were engaged, were energized, and learned a lot about all of the important scientific ideas in the unit. The five groups chose to study ants, dolphins, lions, wolves, and killer whales. No one chose prairie dogs.

One time when I was working with a group of high school teachers, a drama teacher wondered if choice might help with an upcoming project. His students were about to create their own version of *Hamlet*. Their work needed to be inspired by the Shakespearean original but also needed to have its own flavor and some original twists. One of the challenges of the project was the initial intake of the play—all students needed to understand the story in order to participate in the adaptation. As a bit of a purist, his default was to require all students to read the original play. This was problematic because even though all students were competent readers, the original text was a bit too complex for some. He also knew that some students had really heavy course loads and many after-school commitments; because the reading had to be done outside of class, he wasn't sure how thoroughly all students read the text, which then limited their participation in the rewrite. I asked him if he had any different versions of the play, and as it turned out, in addition to the original, he also had an annotated edition. He decided to make both available and allow students to choose the one they thought was the best fit for them—both in terms of comprehension and time. This was a great fit because each choice allowed students to read the play and be prepared to move forward with the class project. Figure 5.1 highlights some other examples of choices that are a good match for the content.

5.1 Choices That Match Content Goals		
Grade	Content	Good Choices
1	Music: rhythm	Students will practice through clapping, stomping, or patting knees.
3	Math: polygons	Students will create examples (for class bulletin board) of triangles, quadrilaterals, or pentagons.
6	Health: effects of drugs	Choose a category to research: depressants, stimulants, or hallucinogens.
8	Science: Newton's Third Law of Motion	To learn the basic principle for homework, students may read an article, watch a video, or do both.
11	Physical education: healthy lifestyles	As part of a personalized self-created healthy living plan, students choose one area of nutrition on which to focus: water, carbohydrates, protein, fats, vitamins, or minerals.

Process Goals

Of course, content is rarely, if ever, separate from process, so in addition to considering choices that match *what* students are learning, you should also consider *how* and *to what degree* they are learning. Are students practicing a skill or trying to memorize content? If so, choices should likely involve practice and repetition. Are students preparing for a class discussion? If so, each option should probably require note taking of some kind to help students record their thinking. This was one of the problems with Christine's sun project—the process of coloring the sun didn't match the learning goals of deepening understanding and preparing to share learning. I remember making a similar mistake once in a math class. After teaching a lesson on reducing fractions, I gave students a few choices for how to practice: They could complete problems in their workbook, create their own problems to practice, or draw a visual representation of reducing fractions. Through this third choice, I was trying to reach out to students who learn visually and might get excited about using colored pencils or markers to draw fractions. The problem was that drawing pictures of fractions takes a while. Students who chose to work in the workbook or create their own problems got a lot of repetition. The students who chose to draw only had time for a few and didn't get much practice—that choice matched the content goal but not the process one.

Here's an example of a choice that matched both content and process. Nate Grove's 8th grade social studies class at Oyster River Middle School in Durham, New Hampshire, had spent weeks analyzing the causes of the American Revolution as they explored the essential question, "Was the American Revolution reasonable?" As a final assessment, each student would formulate an argument (defined as "a civil exchange of reasonable ideas in order to better be able to understand the truth") about whether or not the war was reasonable. In previous years, Nate's students had all written a position paper, but he suspected that some didn't put forth as much effort as they could, thereby limiting how well he could assess their knowledge and understanding. So this year, in addition to getting a problem or example choice (choosing three of eight given events or ideas), students also had a project choice:

• **Art.** Create a side-by-side piece that clearly lays out both sides of the argument and allows the viewer to understand the position you are taking. You must include a written artist statement explaining your choice of images and how they support your position.

• **Museum-style curation.** Create a display of three-dimensional artifacts that clearly explains both sides of the argument and allows the viewer to understand the position you are taking. Your museum pieces must include placards explaining why you created the artifacts and how they support your position.

• **Position paper.** Write a paper that considers three of the events from both points of view and takes a position regarding the central question ("Was the Revolution reasonable?"). Use specific and relevant evidence and examples.

Students had one class period to consider their choices and begin to sketch their initial plans and then three more class periods to complete their work. Upon reflecting on this experience, Nate was convinced that overall students worked harder than they had in previous years. Importantly, all three of these options also allowed Nate to gain a deep understanding of students' knowledge and understanding of the American Revolution, as well as their abilities to craft an effective position statement. Figure 5.2 highlights some other examples of choices that are a good match for the process goals.

5.2 Choices That Match Process Goals		
Grade	**Process**	**Good Choices**
K	Practice counting by 2s	Students will use either discs, plastic insects, or tally marks to practice counting by 2s.
4	Deepen understanding of character traits	Students will choose one character from a recent book they've read and create a labeled poster, write a character sketch, or conduct a mock interview with the character to think deeply about his or her personality and motivations.
7	Warm-up for a timed run	In PE class, students have 10 minutes to walk briskly, jog lightly, do some light stretching and drills, or do a combination of any of these to prepare for a timed one-mile run.
10	Review to prepare for a class discussion	Students are about to engage in a class debate about effects of climate change. To prepare for the discussion, students have five minutes to either review their notes individually or have a warm-up conversation with a small group.

Choices Should Match Students

In addition to matching curricular goals, good choices should also be a good fit for students. Consider possible choices from the perspective of your learners. In whatever lesson, unit, or activity you are planning, imagine yourself as a student in your class. What is already appealing, and what might be a turn-off? What might be easy or hard? How might choice help make things better? Chapter 2 explored how building relationships with students can help students develop a sense of trust that will allow them to take risks. Now we see another important benefit of getting to know students well: You can then create choices that flow directly out of your knowledge of their interests, strengths, needs, and experiences.

Choices Should Reflect Students' Interests and Strengths

It is the end of the school year, and my students are going to engage in one final research project. Because there isn't one unifying theme, topics are varied and diverse. Still, I am a bit surprised and skeptical when Justin announces his first choice of topics: the human arm. "Not the hand or the shoulder, Mr. A.   from here to here," he states, making chopping motions at his wrist and shoulder. I am inclined to steer Justin in a different direction, but first I ask, "Why the human arm?" He goes on to talk with surprising excitement and animation about questions he has about how the bones and muscles fit together and what makes it all work together. He even already has ideas for projects he might take on, both to learn and to share his learning. Seeing his passion for the topic, and knowing that some of the interest is likely the result of having a father who is a physical therapist, I decide to let him go with it, and it turns out to be an amazing research project. During his 20-minute presentation to the class, he has students feeling their own arms to identify different bones and muscles. He builds a simple model of the human arm out of wood and elastic bands to demonstrate how one set of muscles tightens as the other relaxes. I am amazed at how much there was to know about the human arm.

This is perhaps a bit of an extreme example, but it makes the point. When you know your students' interests and passions—when you understand what makes them tick—you can help create and help them find choices that will pique their interest and light their fires. Here are some other examples of ways teachers might tap into students' interests and passions to craft good choices:

• Kody, a reluctant and struggling reader, spends hours each afternoon skateboarding. His teacher finds books about skateboarding to add to the class library as options for reading workshop.

• Knowing that many students in the class enjoy sports, their algebra teacher sprinkles several sports word problems into the collection of problems from which students will choose as they practice parabolic equations.

• A class is about to work at crafting persuasive essays. To help students choose good topics, the teacher facilitates several class brainstorming sessions to help think of ideas about which students can be passionate.

Choices Should Address Students' Needs and Goals

Aaron Ward teaches 5th grade at Oyster River Middle School. His class has been working for a few days at learning about greatest common factors and least common multiples. Aaron has taught several lessons, students have practiced a bit, and they are in that common awkward spot where some students are solid and others need more practice. So Aaron decides it is time for a consolidation period—where students choose the activity that best fits their learning needs.

He initially sets up three choices that help students tap into their needs as well as their learning preferences. One option is to work on a practice sheet that he created. There are a lot of different problems, some easier and some harder, and students can pick and choose the ones that are just right and provide a good challenge. The second choice is to play a simple game with a classmate. One person flips playing cards (using just the numbered cards), and the partner then tries to find the greatest common factor and least common multiple of the numbers shown. Students record their thinking on a blank piece of paper. The third option is to practice with Aaron. He positions himself at a table near one side of the room with dry erase boards and markers. He gives problems and students solve them. Just as students are getting up to begin their work, two students approach Aaron. "Mr. Ward? You know how we've been working on our theory about how this works? Could we go over to the side board and work on our theory?" Aaron knows that these two students are solid with the content and has a vague idea of the theory they were trying to articulate the day before. "Sure," he replies. "Be ready to share your thinking with the class at the end of the period."

Aaron's students work for a solid 30 minutes with great focus and energy. As an observer, I walk around observing and chatting with students. A group of four girls have all chosen the worksheet and are sitting together at a table in the back of the room. I ask them, "Why did you decide to pick the worksheet?" One replies, "I thought it looked like a fun way to practice, and I didn't feel like playing the game." Another nods, "And I like that you can pick the problems that you want to work on." At one point, Aaron leaves the group that has chosen to work with him as he talks with an adult who has entered the room. I slide over to that group and ask, "Why did you choose to work on this option?" Five of the six said that they are still struggling and want to get some extra help from the teacher. All around the room, I hear the same general acknowledgment; students are choosing options based on what they needed as learners.

Here are some other examples of how teachers might offer choices that match students' needs and goals:

• Early in the year, several students shared that one of their goals for the year was to make new friends and get better at working with others, so their teacher routinely offers choices about whether students work alone, with a partner, or in a trio.

• A teacher lets students choose a comfortable body position for solo work: sitting, standing, or lying on the floor.

• Students are studying for a test. The teacher designates four different practice groups, each focusing on a different part of the test. Students choose the one on which they most need to practice.

• As students learn about perimeter and area, they may either use paper-pencil computation or drawings, whichever best helps them understand the concept as they practice.

Again, you must consider, how well do you know your students? It will be impossible to create options that fit their needs as learners if you don't know what those needs are. The more you keep close tabs on your students through daily interactions and formative assessments—conferences, exit tickets, observations, conversations, and class check-ins—the better you will be able to find options that will help students best meet their needs as learners.

Choices Should Match Students' Development

Having majored in child development as an undergrad, keeping the developmental characteristics of the ages I teach in mind has always informed my teaching. When working with 6-year-olds, most options should involve concrete, hands-on elements. When working with 10-year-olds, options might often include partners or small groups. When working with adolescents, consider options that connect with the world beyond the school walls—tapping into their growing fascination with, and understanding of, local and world issues. There are many texts and resources available about child development that you can explore if you want to dig into this topic more thoroughly. Two that I would particularly recommend are *Theories of Development*, by William Crain (2011), which provides a great overview of many different theorists and theories, and *Yardsticks*, by Chip Wood (2007), a fantastic resource for teachers that takes child development theory and brings it into practice in classrooms.

Whether you tap into specific child development resources or rely on your own knowledge and experience of the ages you teach, connecting with what you know works at certain ages can greatly enhance the effectiveness of choice. Here are just a few examples of what this might look like:

• Knowing that 7-year-olds often prefer to work alone or in very small groups, a teacher often gives students the choice of these configurations during math practice work.

• Knowing that it's typical for students in her grade to be fascinated with nature, a teacher stocks her class library with nonfiction texts about animals, weather, and geology.

• Tapping into his students' tendency to enjoy working with technology, a teacher offers students several options, such as PowerPoint, Prezi, and Tumblr, for sharing their learning with the class through their class website.

Choices Should Match Students' Readiness for Choice

How much experience do your students have with choice? In some schools and districts, choice is woven into the fabric of nearly every classroom. Preschoolers and kindergartners get daily choice about centers to visit, books to read, and games to play; elementary and middle school students get daily choices in many subject areas including complex multi-genre projects; high school students engage in independent studies and power-of-one community service learning projects. In other schools and districts, students may not have much experience at all with choice; most lessons may flow from scripted curricula and programs, and much work is standardized and uniform for all students.

If teachers overwhelm students with too many choices or offer them complex choices before they're ready, students may become confused and overly anxious, leading them to choose the simplest and safest options, or even to simply shut down. Students will get the most out of choice when you match choices to students' readiness and experience with choice. There are several ways you might set students up for success.

• **Know about the year before.** Check with teachers in the grade before yours. Ask about the kinds of choices students experienced and how they handled choice. This will help you know what kinds of choices your students might be ready for, as well as the skills you might begin to teach to help them handle more complex choices.

• **Begin slowly.** At the start of the year, keep choices simple and few in number. For example, students might get to choose between two simple exit tickets at the end of class. Or students might get to choose between using colored pencils or markers to color in bar graphs. This will help students learn how to make effective choices and be ready for more complex ones later in the year.

• **Scaffold choice as students are ready.** A middle school teacher I know begins the year by having all students do the same kind of reading journal entry during the first week of school. On the second week, she introduces a second kind of entry. The third week, students have a choice between the first two. Then everyone tries a new entry, and then they can choose between three. In this way, by the middle of the year, all students have a broad experience with many different types of entries and can handle eight options.

• **Adjust as needed.** As you try offering more choice to your students, you'll get a sense of how much they can handle. You may find that certain times of the year, especially high-stress ones like the holiday season or the end of the year, require you to scale back the number and complexity of choices you offer your students.

When Creating Choices, Consider Outliers

When crafting choices for students, it may seem advisable to come up with options that will resonate with most students, and this is true to a certain extent. Most options should be appealing to most students. However, we should also particularly pay attention to students who don't fit the norm—students who are highly advanced, ones who struggle academically, or ones with quirky interests and abilities. For they are the students who so often struggle to connect with schoolwork. And when they don't connect with work, they don't learn and may become disruptive to the learning of others. In my experience, choice is one of the most powerful vehicles for including all students—for creating classrooms that are truly inclusive.

For example, my very first experiment with independent research came as an attempt to challenge a super high achiever in my classroom. I wanted him to have a chance to really fly with a project, so I challenged all students to take on a "challenge project" about something for which they had passion. Justin took the bait and ran with it. In the final month of school, he read *The Lord of the Rings* and drew a 42-piece pictorial timeline of the story. He then wrote his own 12-page sequel complete with Tolkienesque poetry: "In the mountain he attacked the bearer and won his precious prize. In his ire, he fell into the fire, and met his first demise." Justin was in 4th grade.

This is, of course, just one example. You might provide a listening center option to the class with a struggling reader in mind. You might offer a movement option knowing that you have one particular student who just can't sit still. You might offer the option of sharing with a small group instead of the whole class as you consider a student in your class with social anxiety. Students who are using dice to create addition problems to solve might get to choose between using 2, 3, 4, or 5 dice, which would help accommodate needs on both ends of the spectrum. A student with Down syndrome might benefit from a partner reading activity, so you offer that to the whole class. With all of these examples, although you may craft certain choices with specific students in mind, these choices should be available to everyone. I have often been surprised at students who choose options when I had someone else in mind. Sometimes, your students who are outliers find new connections with classmates through these experiences, and your classrooms become truly more inclusive.

Likewise, the specific students we're thinking of, your students with special needs and interests, still need to be able to choose any of the options you offer. Even though you have Analisa in mind when you offer students the chance to read a very high level text about the Civil War, she still needs to get to read *Shades of Gray* if she thinks that is the best fit. She may have some very good reasons for making a choice that appears too easy, and you need to both trust her judgment and help her learn from the choices she makes. For more on helping students make good choices, see Chapter 6.

A Choice Not to Give

With outliers in mind, I have a suggestion of a choice you *shouldn't* offer your students: the choice of who to work with when engaged in partner or small-group projects. With the best of intentions, many teachers routinely let students choose their work partners, and many of the students usually enjoy this. However, for the ones who don't have an immediate go-to friend, this process can be torture. Even when all students have someone in the room with whom they enjoy working, choosing partners can be uncomfortable. I once observed in a high school classroom where the teacher told the class to create small groups. Students looked around uncomfortably, and eventually sorted themselves, but as two girls walked by me to get materials, I heard one whisper to the other, "Ugh. Choosing partners is the worst part." Though there are always exceptions to any rule, I strongly recommend not allowing students to pick partners. Instead, assign partners and groups, either through a process or structure that enables you to create good groups or randomly, so that students learn to work with everyone else in their classroom.

Choices Should Match Logistics

In addition to thinking about the learning goals and the students themselves as you create options for learning, there's one more important category that has to be a consideration: logistics. The choices you create must reasonably fit within the confines of your schedule, the materials you have, and your classroom spaces. In short, choices need to be manageable for you as well as your students!

Time

A colleague of mine recently shared a story about a time when choice got out of hand. He had wanted to spend a couple of days looking at simple nonfiction writing, so he encouraged students to bring in current events from home, either from the newspaper or printed from the Internet. He had his students brainstorm some ways they might share their articles, and they came up with incredibly creative ideas: put on class plays, create a video reenactment, construct three-dimensional models, and put together multimedia presentations. He got caught up in their enthusiasm and before he knew it, a three-day activity had morphed into a multi-week project. When I talked with him, he was trying to figure out how to scale things back—he just didn't have time for the projects his students had suggested.

As you consider choices, make sure the choices you're offering fit the time you have to work. More appropriate choices for the current event share might have been simple cartoon sketches, oral summaries, or partner chats. If students will have one class period to practice multiplying fractions, the choices should reflect that limited time: playing a computer game, creating their own problems, or quizzing a partner would work, while creating a bulletin board display or making up a board game would not.

Materials and Resources

As you think about how materials and resources affect the choices you give students, consider two questions: How do you make sure your choices reflect the materials you have easy access to? How do you get and manage materials to enhance your students' experiences with choice?

One of the ways to keep choice manageable is to make sure to use materials on hand. If you offer choices that require you to engage in a scavenger hunt around the school—seeking out the paper cutter you know is out there somewhere—you may become discouraged with choice and not offer it as often as you could. Also, you need to make sure the materials you offer as choices are plentiful enough and high quality enough for students to have successful experiences with them. If only four students get to choose one option because there is only a little bit of clay, other students don't have access to the full array of choices and will likely (and justifiably) feel resentful, leading them to not fully engage in whatever option they do end up with. So, for your sake and your students', use what you have on hand. For example, if you have a collection of dry erase boards and markers, those can be a choice for ways to play games or practice a variety of math and literacy skills. If students will need access to technology as part of their choice, schedule that work period when you have computer lab time or when you can sign out the laptop cart.

That being said, when students have access to a wide variety of materials and resources, choice can be more engaging and effective. I know it's probably not necessary to encourage teachers to be pack-rats, but consider keeping your eyes open at flea markets or in discount stores. Invite parents to send in extra art supplies or games that students might use in daily learning. When I was teaching in a school near a casino, I ended up getting donations of playing cards and dice that greatly enriched my teaching of math. I once picked up a huge collection of seashells at a yard sale, and those shells found their way into games, art projects, and posters my students created.

Though having shelves of interesting and exciting materials and resources can greatly improve the kinds of choices you offer, you need to be able to manage those materials well, or chaos may ensue. Make sure you spend time introducing and teaching materials to students before they are options for learning. Gradually introduce materials at the beginning of the year, saving more complex or messier options for later. Keep supplies well organized so they are easy to find and easy to put away, and keep supplies that are off-limits out of sight. When you introduce choices, and the materials that accompany them, slowly and deliberately, you'll build students' capacity for success with choice.

Space

Finally, you should make sure that students have the space needed to be successful with the choices you offer. Although creating a skit might be a wonderful way to both deepen understanding and to share learning about a historical event, in a cramped classroom, there just might not be room for this to be a viable option. Instead, if students want to employ acting as a learning tool, they might conduct a mock interview or record a TV news broadcast.

Also, especially if students are involved in multi-day projects that take up space, it's great to find some storage place for in-process work. You might use a cabinet or a shelf in the room where work can be stashed away. A bulletin board can be used to display in-process work just as it can for finished products. If your space is limited, this is another factor to consider as you create choices for students—make sure to only offer options that work in the space you have.

One way to work around limited space is to use areas beyond your immediate classroom. Hallways, nearby classrooms, the cafeteria (when not in use), and even nearby outdoor spaces might all provide extra work spaces for students who need to spread out to work. Though you may feel a bit nervous about your students spreading beyond your classroom, when fully engaged in the joyful work that accompanies choice, students are more likely to be focused and productive and less likely to become distracted or disruptive.

The Process of Creating Choices

Now that you know that choices should match learning goals, what you know about your learners, and the reality of your logistics, let's explore how you actually go about creating these choices. Fortunately, although there is clearly a lot to think about when deciding what choices might work well, the process for getting there is simple and straightforward.

Determine If Choice Is a Good Fit

Will offering students choices help the learning be better? Will it give students a way to find their zones of proximal development or boost their motivation? If a lesson or activity is already highly engaging and appropriate for all learners, choice is probably not going to add any benefit, and it may actually take away from learning by making things needlessly more complicated. If choice will help students better connect with their learning, then it's time to move forward with planning good choices.

Decide Who Creates the Choices

The next step is deciding who creates the choices: the teacher, the students, or a combination of the two. Most of the time it is most efficient when the teacher creates the choices. Especially when the task at hand is simple and short in duration, this is probably the way to go. If students are all going to practice the same skill at the same time, and you want to give them a few different ways to practice, you should probably be the one to come up with the ideas. You can then create options that match the goal, your learners, and the logistics so that most of the work time is spent engaged in practice, not in figuring out what the choices will be. More than once, when wanting to give my students choice but not having the time to think of ones myself, I've made the mistake of asking the students, "Who has an idea about how we might do this?" only to end up with lots of ideas, many of which didn't work.

An advantage, of course, to having students create choices is that the choices are no longer limited by the thinking and creativity of the teacher; 25 heads are better than one. When choices involve work that has the potential to be highly creative and to last for a more substantial amount of time (several days or more), it might be a good time to have students generate ideas for choice. This can take more management on the teacher's part, for you will still need to set parameters about the choices ("We only have three days for the work, and choices need to involve some form of writing") and make judgment calls about choices students come up with ("I know that throwing a football would be a great way to collect data for a scatter plot graph, but it will take too long and the field is being used for a PE class right now").

A nice middle ground is to have a combined effort, where you offer some choices and give students the chance to come up with some as well. For example, as students revise pieces of writing, you might offer three options for small-group sessions students could join: creating a strong opening, adding rich details, or writing with brevity. You might then ask students, "Is there another revision session you would find helpful?" and add one or two to the list. I will often leave the door open for students to come up with their own ideas, even within fairly limited choice. For example, in an art class, where students are learning still life drawings, I might say, "You can draw any of these three items on the middle table. If you have another idea of an object to draw, check with me individually." Just as happened with Aaron Ward's class, sometimes students will have ideas that you never would have thought to offer that are just what students need to fully engage in learning.

Generate Possibilities

Regardless of who is creating the choices, you or your students, the next step is to generate some possibilities. Given the learning goals as well as the interests, strengths, and needs of the learners, what are some possible choices? Be careful here. It would be easy to overwhelm yourself with vast rich possibilities, but for daily learning, you must be efficient with this process. You don't have time to spend 30 minutes brainstorming 15 different ways for students to prepare for a class discussion or investigate the suffix "tion." With that in mind, here are two starting places to help you generate good choices efficiently.

• **Identify what potential problem you are trying to solve.** Is it differentiation? If you're worried that an assignment might be too easy or too hard for some, you're likely using choice to help students self-differentiate. If so, focus on ideas for choices that increase or decrease complexity or challenge. Is it apathy? If you suspect that some students might find a topic or assignment boring, begin with choices that tap into their interests. By beginning with your purpose for offering choice, you can move forward with options that will provide a good match.

• **Begin with what you have.** Have you taught this lesson in the past? If so, don't reinvent the wheel! Start with what you've already done and think of ways to tweak or amend the activity by giving some choice. Do you have a textbook or workbook that the whole class can use? It might be that you find it uninspiring, but it can still serve as a starting place. Perhaps you can give students two choices: read the article in the textbook or another article you found online. Or students might choose a few of the practice problems from the workbook instead of completing all 30.

When creating choices for more complex work such as long-range projects, it's best to stretch out your idea generation over a few days. You might brainstorm a few ideas each day for several days—your brain will be processing away during the in-between times, and you'll think of ideas you wouldn't have if you tried to do it all in one session. Similarly, when students are generating ideas for choices, you might have them think of ideas over several class periods or as a part of a homework assignment. Not only will this give the initial list of choices a chance to grow, it will give students time to start thinking ahead about what might be a good fit for them.

Narrow Down the Choices

Once you have an initial list of possibilities, it's time to narrow down the list and select the options students will have. For many day-to-day choices, this may not even be necessary. If, for example, you came up with two good ways for students to learn about the coefficient of friction (watch a video or read an article), there's no need to narrow down—you're ready to begin planning. Likewise, if choices are really open-ended, as they might be in a thematic research project, there's also no need to narrow them down.

If, however, there are many possible choices and you need to bring them down to a more manageable number, it's time to select the best ones. Here are a few strategies for figuring out which ideas to keep and which ones to save for another time.

• **Keep the number small.** More choices aren't always better. They can be overwhelming and take too long to explain, giving students less time to work. For everyday choice I suggest keeping the number between 2 and 5.

• **Consider outliers.** Again, think of your students who struggle most to find their place in academic work. Make sure at least one choice will resonate with them.

• **Consider logistics.** Do any of the possible choices feel unrealistic because of time, materials, space, or the amount of preparation needed? If you have enough other reasonable choices, save more elaborate and time-consuming ideas for later.

Conclusion

Do you remember learning to drive a car? Do you remember how much concentration and effort it took to remember all of the details of the process of driving? Just to make a turn at an intersection, you have to signal, bring the car to a stop (in the right place), look for other traffic and remember the rules about who goes first if you both arrived at the same time, check your side and rearview mirrors (just to be sure), accelerate at the proper speed while turning the wheel to make a clean turn, and then pull forward into the correct lane. Now, with practice and experience, you don't even think consciously about all of these steps, they happen automatically.

Clearly, there is a lot to consider when creating good choices for your students. Fortunately, just like driving a car, the more practiced and skilled you become at thinking of everyday student learning in terms of choice, the more automatic it becomes. As a teacher I once worked with said, "Once you start using choice on a regular basis, it just becomes the way you think about teaching. It becomes more intuitive."

Once you have created good choices—ones that will help students self-differentiate and tap into their self-motivation—you can move onto the equally important work of facilitating the work itself. You'll begin by thinking about how you can help students select from the good choices they have in front of them!

CHAPTER 6

Helping Students Choose Well

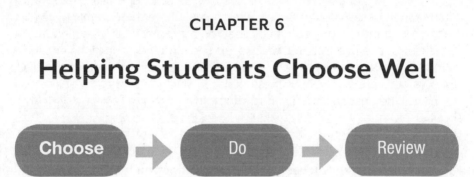

Now that you have crafted good choices for your students, it's time for them to decide what to do, but this involves more than simply saying, "Here are your choices, now pick!" In fact, even as the locus of control shifts from the teacher to the students, you still have an important role to play. You now need to help students choose well. This chapter discusses two main ways to do this. The first has to do with initially setting students up for success with their choices. The second involves helping them when they struggle to make good ones.

Setting Students Up for Success

Consider the example of Patrick Ganz, who teaches high school English in Portsmouth, New Hampshire.

> Every year in Patrick's Literature in Music course, students take on an independent creative project, what they call an "expressional," a term coined by a student one year. Each student chooses a project based on a particular song or genre that was studied. Patrick explains how their expressional must incorporate themes, symbolism, characterization, and other literary devices the class has studied. He offers some initial ideas of projects they might consider, many drawn from

previous years' classes: Create a Facebook page for a character in a song, write and perform their own song in the style of the genre they are studying, create a painting or drawing containing symbols and themes from a song, create a newspaper article related to the events in the song, or choose from multiple other possible projects. Students are encouraged to think of an idea not offered and make their own proposal. Students are also responsible for creating expectation criteria for an assessment rubric. Patrick guides them through this by leading them through the design of a rubric based on a hypothetical project. Watching Patrick introduce this idea to the class, and hearing their questions and ideas as they discuss possible projects and ideas for assessment criteria, I can see students getting excited about these projects while taking them very seriously. He finishes the class by letting students know that they have several days to think about ideas—they will officially make their choices the following week.

As eager as you may be to have students dive right into the work, it's important to set them up for success. Like Patrick did, you want to help students understand their options, build excitement for the work, and give them the time they need to make good choices.

Describe the Choices Well

One of the most important first steps you can take to help students make good choices is to describe the choices well. After all, how will students be able to make appropriate choices—ones that will improve their learning—if they don't understand what each choice entails? For simple choices, this might involve just a short explanation ("To prepare for our class discussion, you have two options. You can either look through your notes from yesterday on your own, or I can partner you up with someone else and you can talk together about yesterday's lesson"). Verbal explanations especially make sense when the choices are few in number and when students are familiar with the choices.

When there are several choices, when the choices are complex, or when some of the choices are new, students will likely need some more support to understand exactly what their options are so they can make an informed decision. There are many ways you might help students out.

• **Visual aid.** A visual aid can help students sort through options. You might post choices on an interactive whiteboard or jot notes on a piece of chart paper. This is especially helpful if the class brainstorms many ideas for choices and you need to keep track of them. You might also show pictures or actual work samples of choices to help students visualize finished products. Keep visual aids posted as students make their decisions.

• **Class discussion.** Like Patrick did with his class, you might have a class discussion to have students ask questions and share ideas about the choices. This can help them deepen their understanding of the options before it's time to choose.

• **Demonstration.** While teaching a math lesson that involved using dice and cards to create math problems to solve, I gave a quick demonstration of each so students could see how they would use either tool. This helped them understand how to use the dice and cards appropriately for the work, but it also gave a brief reminder of the algorithm we were practicing. Especially when you want students to have a clear visual of something they're choosing to do, modeling can be a powerful way to help them understand their choices.

Define "Good" Choices

When students know why they're getting choices and are clear about what they are learning they can better understand how to make good choices. Should students choose an option that's at a particular level of challenge? Are they looking for options that suit their learning style or preference? Are there other factors that will help them make a good choice such as time, materials, or connections to other work? Here are a few examples of teachers helping set students up to make good choices:

• "Today, we're going to start drafting our persuasive writing pieces. As we have been discussing, well-developed persuasive essays have both passion and content. During the past week we have brainstormed a lot of topics, and you've had a chance to try many quick-writes to get your feet wet with some ideas. Now it's time to pick one you want to really develop. There are two criteria for you to consider. First, your topic should be something you care a lot about, so you have great energy and passion for your writing. Secondly, you should have a lot to say about the topic. Lots of ideas will help you write a well-developed essay."

• "To prepare for tomorrow's guest speaker, you're going to generate a list of questions you might ask. It is important for the questions to directly relate to the topic of civil engineering and to come from a place of genuine curiosity. Think about whether you want to generate questions on your own or in a small group. Which of those two options would best help you think?"

• "As you choose a 'just right' book, remember to keep three ideas in mind. First, find a book you want to read—one you'll enjoy. Second, you should be able to read almost all of the words. Third, you should be able to read it smoothly, without big pauses. As you look for books today, keep checking those criteria. Remember that we have those three ideas posted in the class library so you can refer to them as you're browsing."

Guide Students' Thinking, Not Their Choices

Once students understand what choices they have, you can help them think about the choices in ways that will support good decision making. It is here that teachers get to help students work on skills of reflection and meta-cognition. It's important, however, to see your role as helping to guide student thinking, not trying to control the choices they make. This can be a hard balance to strike, especially if you crafted certain choices with specific students in mind. It can be tempting to try and sway their decisions, but as soon as we start to lead students toward a certain choice, we erode their sense of control and may lose their trust. They think, "Ah, I see. There are right and wrong choices, and I'm supposed to figure out what the teacher wants me to 'choose.'" Instead, guide students' thinking, helping them make decisions for themselves. It's a subtle but important distinction. Describe choices in non-judgmental terms and use language that reinforces that students are the ones making the choices (see the examples in Figure 6.1). You may suggest ideas for them to consider, but you should avoid telling them what to do.

Use Empowering Language

When Aaron Ward (whose 5th graders in the previous chapter were practicing least common multiples and greatest common factors) encouraged his students to choose well, he used language that made it very clear who was in charge of the decision: "You know yourselves better than I ever can. Make a choice that will help you learn." When you empower students,

6.1 Suggestions for Guiding Students' Thinking		
Goals	**Instead of . . .**	**Try . . .**
Use description over judgment.	"This choice is easier, and this one is harder." "If you really want a challenge, this one is for you." "I think this is the best choice if you're interested in animals."	"Choice A involves two-digit numbers, and Choice B involves three- and four-digit numbers." "Think about the level of challenge that is the best fit for you." "This choice involves animals."
Use the language of suggestion.	"If you like to move while you work, this is the choice you should pick." "If you need to study homonyms, this is the choice for you." "Meagan, you should pick X."	"If you like to move while you work, you might consider a choice that involves movement." "If you most need to work on homonyms, this one might be for you." "Meagan, which one seems like a good fit to you?"
Use language that encourages metacognition.	"Make a good choice."	"Think about yourself as a mathematician. What best helps you learn?"

putting them in control of their choices, you are showing trust and faith in them and their abilities. Just think about how that feels for students and how that will help them take charge of their own learning! When students hear, "You're in charge of your learning, so think about a choice that is good for you," or "Make sure to find a choice that fits what you need as a learner right now," they will be more likely to make good choices and be truly engaged with their work.

Give Students Time to Think and a Way to Process

As a general rule, the amount of time students need to consider their choices should be proportional to the amount of time they will work. If students are choosing a topic to research over the course of a six-week unit, they should have several days to find a great topic. If students are choosing which math game to play for 30 minutes, once they know their options, a minute to consider is probably enough. For short choices that are relatively simple, consider using some of the following strategies:

• **Silent reflection.** "You're going to have 60 seconds to think to yourselves quietly. Decide which choice you think is the best fit for you."

• **Partner chat.** "Turn and talk with someone next to you. Talk about the choices you have and share with each other which one you're planning on picking. Explain why you're planning to choose that option."

• **Journal writing.** "Now that you've heard about the three different possible writing topics for today, we're going to use writing to consider which ones are best for you. In your journal, explain which choice you're leaning toward and why."

• **Brief class discussion.** "Now that you've heard about the four choices you have, let's think together about them. What are some reasons some people might want to choose each of these options?"

For choices that are more complex—especially ones involving open-ended choices or long-range work such as book groups or research projects—more in-depth strategies that help students process more complex information are helpful.

• **The process of elimination.** Help students narrow down possibilities. When given 10 possible options, students might begin by choosing their top five or three. The process of elimination can also help students when choices are overwhelming. If there are 10 possible options from which to choose, are there some that clearly aren't good choices? Give students a paper list of choices and have them cross ones off that aren't good choices for them. Then have them choose from the remaining ones.

• **Pros and cons.** Once complex choices have been narrowed down to a more manageable number, students can create a t-chart of pros and cons to help them weigh their options. If the pros and cons list gets overwhelming, have students highlight the one or two most important items on each side and use these to help make their decision.

• **Think in categories.** If options are open-ended, like choosing books in a reading workshop or finding a specific topic to study within a theme, have students think of categories to get them started. "Do you want to study a person, place, or event?" "What genres do you especially prefer—historical fiction, fantasy, others?"

• **Prioritizing.** When choices involve multiple variables, not all of which align, students might need to prioritize in order to make a good choice. For example, students might have several reasons to choose a musical instrument to play in the school band: they already know how to play the trumpet, they've always been interested in trying the drums and percussion instruments, one student's older sister played the saxophone, and so on. Have students list all of their reasons and then reorder them with the most important one first and least important last. The list can help them make their choice.

Avoid Over-Structuring

Many teachers wonder about the importance of record-keeping when it comes to choice. Do students need to sign up to show what choice they have made? Do teachers need to keep track of everyone's choices? In my experience, you often don't need to keep track of who is choosing what. Especially in primary grades, it is common for teachers to over-structure this part of choice, creating choice sign-up boards or creating other elaborate systems for students to record what choices they make. These systems can sometimes take time away from working and often aren't needed, especially with simple daily choice. My recommendation is to do this only when it serves a real purpose. If, for example, students are all reading a variety of articles, and you want students to share with someone who read a different article, you might have students sign up using sticky notes on a chart so you can create new groups. Or, if choices involve complex criteria and you will be coaching and helping students come to a final decision, you might have students fill in a choice proposal form so you can understand students' thinking and communicate effectively with them.

Another common way teachers may over-structure choice is through arbitrarily designating that the same number of students need to choose each option. (There are 25 students and five choices, so each choice needs to have five students.) Although that might seem nice and tidy, if you set up this kind of system, invariably, some students won't really get to choose. It should be okay if 21 students choose one option and no one chooses another.

Carefully considering many ways to set students up for success with making good choices can take some time, but it is well worth the effort. In the short term, you are setting students up to do more productive work and to learn more effectively. More importantly though, you are teaching students how to be thoughtful decision makers. You're boosting their skills of self-reflection and metacognition and helping them grow into true learners.

Supporting Students When They Struggle

Rachel comes to you with her list of top choices for topics to study about the Civil War: fashion and clothing, horses, and bugle calls. None of these will help her better understand the essential questions of the unit.

Timmy has been staring at his list of poems for more than 10 minutes, and tears are welling up in his eyes. "I just don't know which one to work on!" he cries in frustration. "Just tell me what to do!"

You watch Mariah, who you know should choose the simplest and most concrete math choice, pick up the option involving complex problem-solving and head back to her seat.

A whole class of young adolescents, despite your great efforts, continue to fixate on who they want to work with instead of what work is best for each of them. As they head to lunch, you hear several of them planning together which books they'll request for the upcoming book group so that they can be together.

Despite teachers' best efforts to set students up for success with making good choices, some students will still struggle. No matter how well you create inclusive and purposeful choices, no matter how well you describe choices and give students the appropriate time and guidance needed to make good ones, some students will continue to need extra support. So, let's consider some ideas for helping students when they struggle to make good choices.

The first is all about coaching students individually, and the second is about whole-class challenges.

Individual Coaching

Students may struggle with making good choices in a variety of ways and for a variety of reasons. When they do, a one-on-one coaching session may be helpful. Like an academic conference, where the goal is to diagnose the problem and then support the student accordingly, these coaching sessions must be individually tailored to the students and their challenge. And even though each student and challenge is a bit different, there are some common problems that seem to arise more often than others.

"I don't know what to choose!" This is especially common for students who haven't had lots of experiences with choice. When students have always been told what to do and how to do it, some freedom and autonomy can be a little scary. For students who have become overly dependent on adults, it may take some time and practice for them to get the hang of feeling comfortable and confident with choice. When students are struggling with choice because they're nervous they might pick poorly, what they most likely need is encouragement. "Trust yourself! Think about what you need and go with it." Or "Try one that you think might work. If it doesn't, that's okay, you can try a different one another time." You might also help them narrow down the options. "Of the five choices, which two are you considering?" Give these students a bit more time on their own, and resist the urge to rush in and save them ("Why don't you try this one?"). Students will gain confidence with experience and practice.

"I don't like any of these choices!" Sometimes students balk at the choices given. It may be that they really don't like the choices, or it may be that they're worried about being able to do well. They might just be having a bad day and are struggling with work in general—any choice won't be the right one in this moment. If this is coming from a place of genuine disinterest, you might challenge the student to come up with another idea—one that still fits that learning goal and that will be a good personal fit. If, however, a student is pushing back against any and all choices, you may need to help them move forward. Like in the above example, you might narrow choices down, but do so in a more direct way: "Choose between these two." Or, if necessary, you might make the choice for them, knowing that there will be many more opportunities at other times for them to practice making choices.

"Is this graded?" or "Is this going to be on the test?" These types of questions are most common in upper grade settings where traditional testing and grading structures are the norm. As disheartening as these questions may be, remember that students are only playing the game they've been taught to play. They have been trained to consider work through the lens of hoop-jumping, and a shift toward more authentic learning goals doesn't just happen overnight.

First, answer their questions in a straightforward manner. "No. You're not being graded on this assignment." "Yes. The content we're working on will be a part of the summative assessment that we're having on Friday." A strategy that can then help these students move forward with good choice-making is to bring them back to the learning goals. "So, think about the learning goal. Your goal is to practice conjugating these three verbs and using them in authentic sentences. Which of the three choices do you think will help you get there?" When tests and grades are a reflection of learning instead of the actual goal, students can learn to make choices based on their individual learning needs.

"I know what I'm going to choose!" (But we think they're wrong.) There will be times when students will make poor choices. They will choose options that are too hard or too easy. They will pick things that they actually don't find interesting. They will make mistakes. This is good. After all, if students aren't making mistakes, they aren't learning. Imagine trying to learn a new language without ever mispronouncing a word or learning to ride a bicycle without falling over. So, what should you do? It depends.

When the assignment is short, and the long-term impact of a poor choice is minimal, it's probably best to do nothing. Let students try their choices and learn from experience. After sitting with a book they can't read or a math exercise that's too easy, they'll likely realize they've made a mistake and self-correct. Or it might be that they actually knew themselves better than you did and they made the right choice after all. If a student was up half the night taking care of a sick parent or sibling, he or she might need to work on a choice that would normally be on the easy side, just to get through the day.

When an assignment is long or complex, making a poor choice can have a bigger negative impact on learning. Choosing a book for a three-week book group that is too hard will result in a student who doesn't get the reading practice needed and will diminish the learning of others in the group. Choosing a research topic that won't work could result in weeks of frustration and low learning. One of my 5th graders once wanted to study the Korean War as a part of a social studies theme about conflict in U.S. history. Her grandfather fought in the war—a fantastic reason for wanting to learn more about it. This was when the Internet was still in its infancy and most research resources had to come in print form. It wasn't until we were far enough into the unit that she couldn't reasonably switch to another topic that we both realized that there weren't many resources on the conflict that she could read independently. I had to sit with this student and read and interpret encyclopedia entries, which limited how much she could learn (not to mention how well I could work with other students).

This would have been a great time to exercise my veto power. Used only on occasions when the negative impacts of a poor choice are too great to bear, you may need to tell students that they can't make a particular choice and help them find a better alternative.

Whole-Class Teaching

The above ideas may help students who are struggling individually, but what about when a whole class, or at least a whole group of students, is having a hard time choosing well? Again, you should expect that this will be the case. And just like you do when individual students struggle, you should view these struggles as natural and positive—they are opportunities to teach small-group or whole-class lessons to help students gain the skills they need to become more self-reliant, independent, and autonomous learners.

Many of the strategies and struggles discussed in the previous section may well apply to whole-group settings, but let's take one and play around a little, considering how you might help a whole class. For the sake of an example, let's think about how to support a group of adolescents who are paying more attention to who is doing what than they are to their own individual needs and preferences.

Ms. Wallace has watched her students switch places in a circle as students are counting off by threes, quickly calculating where they should stand to get grouped with their buddies. She has watched students exchange nods and knowing looks with each other as soon as her directions seem to indicate that students might get to work with a partner. And now, she wants to give her students the chance to choose a novel to read in literature circles. Each book is set during the American Civil War. In addition to exploring this historical event, students will examine elements of historical fiction, such as how an author blends real historical events into a fictional tale. Ms. Wallace wants to help students develop their skills of effective decision making, especially to move away from using peer pairings as the only criteria. She begins by stating the objective clearly to the class: "You are soon going to choose a book to explore as part of a literature group. Making a decision like this can be complex—there might be many different reasons you might pick one book over another. Together, we're going to think of some ideas and work on some strategies to be thoughtful as you choose a book."

Next, she leads a class brainstorming session: "You'll get to see the books in a little while. First, let's just think about reasons you might pick one book over another. What are some ideas you have?"

The class generates an interesting and varied list: the topic or content of the book, the gender of the main character(s), how interesting the cover looks, how challenging the book looks, the length of the book, and whether someone has already read the book or not were a few. There are also some questions that arise that help the teacher explain the parameters of the book study. One student asks, "Can we pick the same book as our friends?" Ms. Wallace explains that students should put down their top two choices for books on cards and that she will create the groups. Students may end up in a group with friends, but it isn't a sure thing. Another student asks if the books will be read in school or at home. The teacher explains that much of the reading will happen at school, though some might need to be done at home as well so that everyone is ready to discuss chapters at the same time.

Now that the class has a list of reasons they might consider as they choose a book, Ms. Wallace leads them through a prioritization exercise. "Look at this list of reasons you came up with. Decisions can be hard to make when there are an overwhelming number of reasons. One strategy that can help is to prioritize.

So now you're going to choose the top four reasons you might use to choose a book. As you look at this list, which reasons are most important to you?" Students record these four reasons on a piece of paper. "Now number these reasons from 1 to 4. A 1 is your most important reason, and a 4 is your fourth most important reason. Really think about what is most important to you." Ms. Wallace is pleased to see that although who else was reading the book appears on many students' lists, it isn't first on most of them.

Now students are ready to start exploring the four book choices. Students get a few minutes with each book. They read the backs, look at the covers, and flip through the pages, jotting notes about each book to help them remember details for when they choose. After students have explored all four books, Ms. Wallace leads them through the last part of the process. "Now it's time to choose. Look back at your four reasons for choosing a book, especially thinking about your top one or two reasons. Think about each book, and review the notes you took. Write your name on this note card then write down your top two book choices. I'll collect these and create groups, and we'll get started with our book groups tomorrow!"

When given the chance to think and plan ahead, students were able to be more objective and rational than when the choice came with little time to process and think.

Conclusion

Helping students choose well is perhaps one of the most important and yet overlooked aspects of giving students choices in school. Too often, students are given choices without any support or guidance about how to choose. We shouldn't be surprised when they struggle. Fortunately, the payoffs of teaching students how to choose well are immense. In the short term, students are able to find learning options that are a good fit, enabling them to learn the content at hand or practice the skills of the moment with more purpose, passion, and competence. There are benefits that go way beyond the Pythagorean Theorem and writing in complete sentences; students are learning skills of self-reflection and decision making that can be used throughout their lives.

CHAPTER 7

Facilitating Choice Work:
Leading Great Learning

It might be easy to assume that once you have crafted great choices and students have chosen what to do, the role of the teacher diminishes. I remember as a new teacher hearing about the difference between being a "sage on the stage" and a "guide on the side." Having suffered through years of lecture-based teaching, I knew that I didn't want to be the former, so I immediately identified with the latter. I loved the idea of a child-centered classroom—one where the teacher set up exciting experiences and then set the students loose to explore and learn on their own. I knew that I wasn't going to be kicking back with a cup of coffee and a newspaper or grading papers at my desk while students worked at theirs, yet I hadn't fully realized how dynamic and important the teacher is when the class is engaged in student-centered work. The term "guide on the side" is way too passive. There is nothing "on the side" about facilitating student-centered learning. In fact, a better term might be "coach in the middle."

Once students are working, especially when the work is diverse and they are in their zones of proximal development, the teacher is more important than ever. Teachers must help keep a dynamic learning environment running smoothly, offer differentiated support to students involved in diverse work, keep tabs on how everyone is doing, and troubleshoot as problems arise (as they inevitably will). This chapter will explore many of these roles and offer strategies for facilitating the "do" phase of choice effectively.

Teacher as Coach

Your most important role to play, as students are involved in the "doing" part of the choice, is that of coach. This is where you offer students the individual and small-group attention and instruction that help them grow the most. Remember, the zone of proximal development is an area where great growth can happen because it is a place of stretching—of being in a space where you need hard work and support to be successful. If your students place themselves in this space, they will need your help!

Many teachers have expressed to me the concern that they won't have time for coaching because their students need so much direction (and redirection). "I can't help the ones who need help when they're all doing the same thing at the same time. I have to spend so much time telling kids to sit down and get back to work or managing students who are disrupting others. How will I ever be able to coach effectively if the work is even more diverse?" This is a valid concern, but there's something important to remember about choice, which can help ease it. When students are engaged in choice—when they find work that is interesting, fun, and appropriately challenging—they are more on task. They're less likely to wander around the room, stare blankly out the window, or start bothering someone nearby, because they're invested in the work itself. This frees you from the role of classroom manager and helps you spend more time in the role of academic coach.

With that in mind, let's think about some of the skills we should practice and strategies we should employ to coach students well.

Be an Expert Observer

Hayden has been sitting at his seat for five minutes and has yet to start writing. His teacher notices that color is creeping up the back of his neck and his fists are clenched—both signs that his frustration is building. His teacher slides over to Hayden and ventures, "How's it going, Hayden?"

It would be impossible to be a great coach without keen skills of observation. This is vitally important as we facilitate work that happens during choice. As students engage in work that is more diverse, we can't rely on glancing at the work alone to determine how students are doing—we have to pay more attention to the students. This means making time during work periods to watch students as they work to notice their facial expressions as they are engaged, excited, bored, and frustrated. This helps us better know them so we can give them the right kind of support.

Offer the Right Kind of Support

Gretchen has been working on a math sheet and is clearly solid with the skill. She zooms through problem after problem, barely thinking. Next to her is Carradine who is clearly struggling, doing more erasing than writing, and looking upset. Nearby is Jake who is completely absorbed in his work. He is so focused that he barely seems to notice as you pull up a chair at their table. Each of these students likely needs a different kind of support.

Gretchen probably needs a push: "Gretchen, it looks like you're really solid with this and it isn't providing much of a challenge for you. Let me try giving you a couple of problems to try that might be more fun." Carradine needs some support: "Carradine, you look frustrated. How can I help you out?" Jake needs to be left alone. If he's completely engaged in appropriately challenging work, we don't want to mess that up.

There are, of course, many different strategies you might use to help support students as you coach them. There are four that I think are especially important tools to use to help support students in the zone of proximal development.

• **Ask open-ended questions.** "How do you think your work is going so far?" "What is something you're proud of, and what's something you're hoping to improve?" "What are some questions you have about your work?" Open-ended questions like these can help students deepen their thinking about their work and can help build their skills of self-reflection and metacognition.

These are especially good questions to use when first engaging with students in a coaching session to jump-start conversations and help you understand where you might focus your attention.

• **Offer encouragement.** Offering students concrete positive feedback about their work can help them both recognize their strengths and gain a boost of momentum to push through challenges. Unlike praise, encouragement is about offering feedback, not showing approval. "John, I know you've been working at developing this character. It's really coming along. He's really growing and changing through the story!" "Eliza, the colors you've used on this PowerPoint presentation really help highlight the content. They're bold enough to stand out, but they don't take the attention away from what you want to say."

• **Reinforce student ownership.** When coaching students, make sure they maintain both physical and emotional control of the work. As much as possible, they should hold the paper and the pencil. They should mark corrections or notes in the margins. The work should face them as you confer. You can also use language that emphasizes their ownership of the work: "What can I do to support you with your work?" Use the word "you" more than "I." Instead of "I think you should . . ." say, "You might consider . . ."

• **Offer the right amount of support.** You might sit down to help a student with a project they're working on and see seven or eight things right away that could be better. If you overwhelm students with too many suggestions, not only will they not be able to remember everything you suggest, they may become discouraged, which could decrease their motivation. Usually, just one or two suggestions at a time is plenty for a student to consider. Once they are ready, you might then focus on another suggestion or two.

Consider When to Let Students Change Their Choice

Fifteen minutes into the science work period, Jamal comes to you looking frustrated. "I chose an experiment, but it's not as fun as I thought. Can I change to another one?" You're worried that he won't have time to complete a different experiment. On the other hand, if he's not interested in the one he's working on, how much will he learn? What do you do? Do you let him switch or not?

There's no single simple right answer to whether or not to let students change—it's highly contextual and will depend on the nature of the work and the needs of the student. A great place to start is to ask the students why they want to change. They may have a great reason for switching that never would have occurred to you, or you may get the sense that they're struggling with something and need some coaching. Sometimes, it will be perfectly fine for students to change their mind. Mark's been practicing one kind of punctuation for 10 minutes and feels like he has mastered it and wants to move on to practice another—why not let him change? On the other hand, Josie, who chooses one book to read as a part of a group, probably can't easily switch to another halfway through. Not only does she have a group counting on her for participation, but to join another group midway through might be disruptive (not to mention she would have to read half of the new book to catch up). You'll also find that there are some students who seem to request choice changes too often, and this may have to do with challenges in following through or finishing work.

What's more important than knowing exactly how to handle every request is that you have the right mindset about choice changes. If we're rigid and overly authoritarian, never letting students change, we're probably limiting students' learning at times and robbing them of chances to make better decisions. If, on the other hand, we allow any and all changes, some students may struggle with sticking with choices, and they may not get their work done.

Managing Work Periods

When the whole class is doing the same thing at the same time, classroom management often is fairly straightforward, simple, and reactive: As students get off track, teachers push them back on. (When the work is particularly boring, it may feel like we're playing Whack-A-Mole at the county fair.) As students engage in more diverse work, more proactive management strategies are required so that students can function more independently. We need to set students up for success with independence so they can keep themselves on track.

Systems That Support Independence

In Moharimet School, in Madbury, New Hampshire, Trisha Hall's 1st graders are transitioning from a literacy lesson in the circle to independent work time. It is January, and Trisha has invested a lot of time at the beginning of the year teaching student routines of independence, so these students know just what to do. They move with energy and purpose to various places in the room, each carrying a plastic tote that houses reading, writing, and word study materials. Several students immediately get their writing pieces and meet with Trisha at a kidney shaped table—they are first up for a small-group lesson on editing for punctuation. Many students begin with independent reading and hunker down into bean bag chairs or lie on the floor with a book. Three students move directly to the listening station, put on headphones, and open up books together. A parent volunteer in the classroom sits at a side table and calls students over one at a time to work on individual vocabulary words that students have written in their reading logs. Two pairs of students sit down together to read aloud to each other quietly.

As I sit and observe, I'm astounded by these 6- and 7-year-olds' independence. They get supplies independently, sit in appropriate work spots around the room, and easily transition from word study to reading to writing as needed, checking off boxes on their individual schedule cards as they work. Several students use the library sign-out sheet to visit the school library to get new books. First, they check the sheet to make sure no one else is out of the room. Then they write their name on the next line. When they head back from the library, they cross their name off the sheet. Trisha works with several small groups throughout this literacy block, occasionally stopping to help a student in the room get back on track, but it's incredible to see how productive students are as they engage in various and diverse literacy work.

As you use choice in your daily teaching—especially more complex choice where students are working on projects or long-term work—you will need to create and teach systems that allow students to be more independent. If Trisha is trying to work with a small group but a long line of students is waiting to ask her questions ("Where are the pens?" "Can I get another book?" "Do I have to work on word study today?" "Can I go to the bathroom?"), she won't be able to coach the students who need her academic support in the moment. Though different systems will be needed and will look different at different grades, the following ideas might get you started.

• **Nonacademic logistics.** How will students take care of logistics that don't have anything to do with schoolwork? The fewer logistical questions you need to answer the more time you have to work with students. Have sign-out sheets near the door so students can leave and reenter the room on their own. Place a box of Band-Aids in an easy-to-reach locale. Have a schedule displayed so students know what is coming next and when. Consider other common non-academic questions that arise in your room and think of ways to help students take care of these things more independently.

• **Daily work.** Where will students keep materials and in-process work? Trisha uses totes (stored on a shelf when not in use) to organize literacy work, and I used large Ziploc bags that would fit into students' cubbies. Middle and high school classes can use shelving units to keep various classes' work organized and neat so it's easy to access. Also, having a designated spot for finished work can help students pass in work when it's time.

• **Supplies.** Teach students how to access, use, and put away materials. Introduce materials gradually as the year unfolds so students are able to learn these routines without being overwhelmed. Keep supplies that aren't needed or off-limits out of sight.

• **Transitions.** Teach and practice systems to help students settle into work and then clean up efficiently. Also help students know what options are available if they finish a piece of work or are waiting for help.

• **Keeping track of progress.** For larger, longer multi-step projects, students often benefit from having a checklist or other tool that helps them break down the larger work into smaller, more manageable steps. This can keep them moving through a complex process more independently while also making it easier for you to touch base and see how they're doing.

One last piece of advice about systems: be careful not to over-systematize! Sign out sheets, charts to show work completion, and the like are all well and good, insofar as they help facilitate independence. If they aren't necessary, however, they're just more work, so make sure only to use systems that are needed.

Time Management

One of the greatest perceived challenges for teachers of managing choice work involves time. It's hard enough to keep a whole class together when the work is the same—isn't it worse when students are engaged in different work tasks at once? I've found that it's no worse than any other work period, and with one simple shift in time management, it can actually be easier.

Here's the shift, and it involves letting go of an unwritten (and maybe even unconscious) assumption many have about work: that good work is all about finishing a task. Instead of framing work periods around finishing work, try framing them around amount of time. For example, if students have three different worksheets from which to choose, instead of requiring all students to finish the one they choose (which would create a time challenge even if they all did the same one), simply have students all work for the same amount of time. If one student finishes half of one sheet while another has time to get through two of the three choices, that's fine. It's all part of the differentiation built into choice. In this way, instead of rushing to finish or feeling inadequate because they're working slower than others, students can relax into the work and focus on the quality, not quantity, of what they're doing.

Another important aspect of time management to keep in mind is remembering to save time at the end of the choice process for the "review" stage. When students are working well and you're wrapped up in coaching sessions, it can be easy for time to slide by, and then before you realize it you're late for lunch. Try setting a timer, or designate a student reminder to help set aside the time needed to reflect on work before moving on to the next period. Give students a few minutes heads-up before transitioning to this time so they can get to a good stopping place in their work.

Managing the Class While Coaching

Even when students are highly engaged in their work, some students will still need support with staying on track. Students may drift off task, get frustrated and need to calm down, or get in someone else's space, causing tension. Though using choice reduces classroom misbehaviors, it certainly doesn't eliminate them, so you will still need to manage the class as a whole as you coach. Here are a few tips for managing these complex work times.

• **Face the class.** One of the keys to effective observation is your own body position. When working with individual students and small groups, position yourself so that you are facing as many other students as possible. Ideally, you would also be able to see the classroom door easily to see if anyone is coming or going.

• **Scan the class.** When working with students, periodically scan the rest of the class. Even if you sweep your eyes across the room for one second, you can usually get a quick read on how things are going and begin to assess any potential challenges. A small group of students is giggling together at a table. Are they simply enjoying a light moment, or are they off task? Andrew's head is down on his table. Is he thinking, taking a brief rest, or discouraged and disconnecting?

• **Pay attention to students' eyes.** One way to keep your scans efficient is to look at students' eyes. Are they focused on work or the task at hand? Do they look engaged? Bored? Upset? Mischievous?

• **Decide when to act.** Many times, students who get off track pull themselves right back to work quickly (especially when they're enjoying their work—as they're likely to do when they've had some choice!), so there's no need to intervene. On the other hand, if small misbehaviors snowball and you wait too long to redirect and support, it can be harder to get things back on track. A brief, firm, kind redirection can often do the trick—helping students reengage with minimal disruption. Or you might decide that it's time to end the work period, as you see students run out of steam.

Students as Peer Supports

One of the great benefits of choice is that students can be more collaborative (and less competitive) than when all students are doing the same thing at the same time, because all are more focused on their own work and can't easily compare it to others'. This makes it easier for students to help each other out. This is fortunate because as the work gets more diverse it is harder for a single adult to meet all students' needs.

However, it's important to do more than simply say to students, "Help each other out." After all, coaching is hard, and, as you know if you've ever observed and offered feedback to a colleague, peer coaching is even harder. To set students up for success, you must give them the needed structures and supports so they can offer (and receive) meaningful feedback.

Peer Support Systems

One of the ways to help set students up for success with peer coaching is to create systems that help structure peer conversations and conferences. Introduce these kinds of systems gradually, erring on the side of safety early in the year, moving to more complex structures later in the year as students are ready.

Structured partner chats. Early in the year, you can have students practice simple partner chats, helping them practice having collegial conversations. These partner chats are then a vehicle for highly structured peer feedback conferences where you give a prompt and a short amount of time to talk. Here are some prompts that will help students practice how to give and receive peer feedback:

- **One positive.** "Make one positive comment about your partner's piece of work."
- **Tell me more about.** "Help your partner go deeper with their work by finishing the prompt, "Tell me more about . . ."
- **Three plusses and a push.** "On a sticky note, write down three things your partner is doing well with her work. Then offer her one suggestion—a push to help her improve her work."

When these kinds of safe and structured peer conferences are built right into choice work periods, all students get to practice, and get comfortable with, offering and receiving peer input. My suggestion is to use these brief partner chats frequently—even daily—early in the year. Students will build their skills so they can engage in richer and more meaningful peer supports later in the year, when the work is more challenging.

Peer conference sign up. One of my favorite ways to help students help each other is to create a system for students to connect for a conference. This system can work well whether students are involved in a long-range project or just a short class period activity.

Create a simple chart where students can write their name and a brief note about their struggle. If other students see their struggle and think they might be able to help, they cross off the name and move in for a conference. During research or writing workshops, I often had a chart that included a column for teacher conference as well as a peer conference request. In this way, students could take charge of their own learning (by requesting support) and help each other through many of the minor struggles that slowed learning. I was then able to focus on students who needed to meet with me, so my time was spent more efficiently. It was like we were a class of 25 colleagues, all working together and supporting each other.

Study buddies. Another way to help students help each other is to partner them up so that all have a go-to person to consult with when they need help. You might set up study buddies for just one lesson, either by choosing partners ahead of time who you know might be able to support each other well or by drawing names out of a hat. If students are engaged in a longer-range project, you might set up go-to partners for the duration of the project. One year I experimented with using homework study buddies. Each student had a classmate he could call if he needed a reminder about an assignment or didn't remember exactly what to do.

To be clear, having one go-to classmate doesn't mean that students can't work with anyone else, it just means that they have a designated starting point. Study buddies, or any of the other peer support systems, aren't supposed to replace teacher help—far from it. These systems just help put structures in place so that all students can support each other, right along with the teacher.

Teach Peer Support Skills

Have you ever observed a colleague and experienced how challenging it can be to give supportive constructive feedback? It involves a complex skill set, requiring us to observe well, consider what support to offer, and pay attention to the tone of our delivery. If this is hard for teachers, just imagine how challenging it can be for students!

Basic skills of collaboration. Peer collaboration is most effective when you teach the skills students need to both offer and receive peer support well. Importantly, many of these skills are ones teachers are already responsible for teaching and will support students' academic work whether they are involved in choice or not. Just take a look at a few from the Common Core State Standards in Figure 7.1.

7.1	
Sample Skills of Collaboration	
Standards	**Description**
CCSS, Writing, Grade 7 (W.7.5)	"With some guidance and support from peers and adults, develop and strengthen writing as needed by planning, revising, editing, rewriting, or trying a new approach, focusing on how well purpose and audience have been addressed."
CCSS, Speaking and Listening, Grade 3 (SL.3.1)	"Engage effectively in a range of collaborative discussions (one-on-one, in groups, and teacher-led) with diverse partners on *grade 3 topics and texts*, building on others' ideas and expressing their own clearly."
CCSS, Standards for Mathematical Practice (MP3)	"Students at all grades can listen or read the arguments of others, decide whether they make sense, and ask useful questions to clarify or improve the arguments."

Consider some of the specific behaviors and skills you might teach your students so they can engage in successful collaboration:

- Making respectful eye contact
- Using effective body position when conferring
- Asking clear questions
- Accepting feedback politely (and deciding if or how to use it)
- Knowing how to offer help without taking over
- Keeping conferences focused and brief

Modeling and practicing these kinds of skills is a year-long process, so start with the most basic ones that your students need to be successful with beginning collaborative work. You can teach more challenging and in-depth skills as they are ready throughout the year. This is a huge topic, of course, so for a more in-depth exploration of helping students with collaborative work, refer to *Productive Group Work*, by Nancy Frey, Douglas Fisher, and Sandi Everlove (2009). Let's next consider a few skills in particular that can especially help when students are using choice.

Open-ended questions. Open-ended questions can help peers support each other, even when they have different skill sets, are working on different kinds of assignments, or don't even fully understand each other's work. By teaching students how to ask these kinds of questions, you empower the whole class to support and guide each other well.

> Kathryn and Brian are having a writing conference. Brian is, in many ways, a more skilled writer than Kathryn, but he's stuck and needs help moving forward with an essay. Kathryn begins with an open-ended question: "What do you think is going well so far?" Brian explains that he thinks that he makes some good points early in the essay, but then it starts to fizzle out. Kathryn follows up. "Why do you think it's fizzling?" Brian pauses and considers. "I guess I'm not giving many details right now. In my first point, I list a bunch of reasons, and now I'm just listing points." Kathryn continues, "So what do you think you might do next?" Brian nods and says, "I need to take my next points and give reasons for each one. Thanks. I'm all set now!"

One strategy some teachers use to help students as they learn how to use open-ended questions is to post lists of questions that students can use when they confer. This visual reminder of questions to ask can help conferences be more productive. Here are some you might use if you want to try this strategy:

- What's going well so far?
- What might you try next?
- What else have you tried?
- If you could wave your magic wand, what would you change?
- What are some other ideas you have?

Receiving feedback. I have seen student conferences dissolve in frustration as one student offers advice and support and the other refuses to accept any ideas. Students need support in what to do with feedback they receive, especially if they think it won't be helpful. There are many ways students might respond such as saying thank you, asking follow-up questions, or jotting down notes to think about later. Helping students learn how to accept feedback respectfully will set a tone that allows conferences to be productive and positive throughout the year.

Knowing when not to confer. It's easy for students to get so caught up in helping each other that they may neglect their own work, so help students learn that it's okay to not help someone if the time isn't right. You might brainstorm with a class, "Even though we all want to help each other out, there are times when you might have to politely say no or not offer to help someone. Let's think together about that. When are times we shouldn't help a classmate?" Students will come up with great ideas: when you have too much work to do yourself, when you've already helped someone else, when you're really on a roll with your own work and don't want to break your concentration, and others. You can then post this list to help remind students that sometimes it's okay to *not* help a classmate.

Cautions with Peer Support

Students helping too much is just one caution to consider when setting students up to support each other during choice work periods. There are a few others that deserve particular attention.

Watch for problematic interactions. Some students struggle to interact appropriately together. They may get silly or off task, or one may be antagonistic towards another. If you see that some students struggle with positive and productive peer coaching, you might give them extra support when they're together or put them with different partners. This is one of the ways that you help create a learning environment that is safe and respectful—by carefully monitoring student interactions and supporting as needed.

Know the difference between supporting and judging. When students support each other as they work, it's important that the feedback they offer be in the form of helpful suggestions, not criticism or judgment. Students may fill out peer support rubrics for in-process work to help support each other as they work on projects, but they should never grade or conduct summative assessments of each other's work. Students may offer ideas to each other about solving problems, but they should never swap papers and correct each other's work. When peer conferences are about judging, critiquing, and evaluating in this way, many students will no longer feel safe, which will impede their learning.

Be wary of public coaching. Imagine sharing a brief presentation about a unit your students just completed at a staff meeting. At the end of the share, some well-meaning colleagues offer you some feedback: "I like how active your students were, but do you think they were really mastering the content?" "Which standards were you meeting in that unit? I think I saw a few, but I'm not sure." "I have an idea about a way you could make it better next time . . ." What was supposed to be a light and positive share has turned into a critique. I have seen this same thing happen in the classroom. A student shares in front of the class and students, unclear about how to respond, shift from showing support and appreciation to critical feedback.

Receiving supportive feedback requires a degree of vulnerability. This can be hard enough in a one-on-one conference. Given publicly, in front of peers, this kind of feedback, even when delivered gently and with kindness, can hurt. So, as a general rule, avoid public feedback sessions. Make sure to be clear when students share with the class that questions and comments should only be supportive, and give some examples to help the class know what that looks like. If you do want to give students the chance to learn from each other, structure it so it's done privately. For example, to offer a classmate constructive feedback, students might all write one positive comment and one suggestion on a sticky note, allowing the receiver to take a breath and digest information on their own. Even with this form of gentle system, you should move forward with caution and make sure that peer feedback is truly helpful or needed. In the spirit of "do no harm," it might be a practice to reconsider all together.

Conclusion

A good friend and colleague loved to give me a hard time about how chaotic my 4th grade classroom looked when students were working on various tasks at once. Three students might be practicing a skit, four others creating a mural, several more typing on computers, and the rest engaging in various other art projects—all focused on a science unit on geology. Meanwhile, next door in his room, his 5th graders sat in neat rows, working on quiet seatwork—all doing the same thing at the same time. "Anderson!" he would scream in mock horror. "What's going on in here? It looks like Romper Room!"

From his perspective, my room lacked structure. Students were all over the place, and it often had a tone and feel that was both energetic and if not loud, certainly wasn't quiet. I would argue that facilitating learning in classrooms where choice is used actually requires *more structure*. All of the ideas we've explored in this chapter, from teaching how to use and care for various supplies, to helping students learn how to collaborate effectively, to coaching many different students engaged in various kinds of work at once, require a complex set of management and teaching strategies. And this complex work is absolutely worth it when our students come alive with joyful, vigorous, meaningful learning.

CHAPTER 8

The Power of Self-Reflection

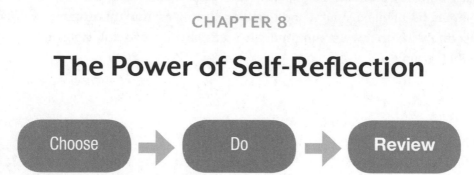

Ms. Booth's 4th graders have been working for 45 straight minutes creating tessellations using various math manipulatives. She has been so busy helping students, and everyone has been so engaged, that the whole class jumps when the afternoon announcements blare over the loudspeaker. "Oh my gosh!" exclaims Ms. Booth. "Everyone put your supplies away, push in your chairs, get your coats, and get ready for dismissal!"

Mr. Hunter is watching the clock. He knows he should have his students review their learning before they change classes, but this group of sophomores and juniors is never this focused, and he doesn't want to mess with a good thing. "We can always reflect tomorrow," he rationalizes.

There are a variety of reasons teachers might neglect the final student phase of choice—the "review" phase. Like Ms. Booth, they might lose track of time, or like Mr. Hunter, they might choose to squeeze every bit of time that they can out of the "do" phase. It could be that a teacher doesn't see the value in having students reflect on their learning. It might even be that it's easy to overvalue the actual work products students produce—the essays, graphs, tests, and projects. Could it be that we sometimes lose sight of what is really important: that students are learning how to learn? It is crucial to recognize that in order to *self-direct*, students must know how to *self-reflect*.

This is one of the most powerful aspects of using choice with students. Choice empowers students to take more control of their learning and invest themselves in their work. Teachers must make sure to help them learn from this experience. After all, when you're fully immersed in work, it can be hard to simultaneously reflect on what you're doing. I'll never forget a student in my class who helped me realize how hard it is to do two things at once. Melissa had been reading aloud to her group—a novel they were exploring together—and she had read beautifully. Her articulation was great, and her voice rose and fell with expression and emotion. When she finished, I exclaimed, "Melissa! That sounded so fluent and expressive! Can you explain what that part of the book was about?" She looked at me incredulously and demanded, "How am I supposed to know what was happening? I was the one *reading it*!"

Students need a chance to step back and reflect on their learning and work, separate from the learning experience itself. Giving students a chance to review the choices they have made and the learning in which they have been engaged is how we do this. We help them better understand themselves as learners, grow in their skills of self-reflection and self-assessment, and help them get better at self-directing their learning in the future. In short, we help our students become better learners.

This means that it's critical to make the "review" phase of the process a priority. Set a timer so you don't lose track of time. Build time for reflecting right into your lesson plans and think ahead about how students will review. Make sure not to fall into the habit of reviewing for the sake of reviewing; make this period of reflection meaningful for students. Though there are many ways to structure this review period, there are a few key types of review to consider.

Types of Review

Before we examine *how* to help students review, let's consider *what* they should review. There are four categories of review to use with students.

Review Choices

When you ask students to reflect on the kinds of choices they made and consider whether or not those choices worked, you're helping them grow in skills of effective decision making. You are also reinforcing students' power and control of their learning. You send the message that "You're going to get to choose again, so keep thinking about how to get the most out of your learning!" Having students get better at making good choices also enables everyone to engage in more complex and interesting choices later in the year. Here are some examples of questions to help students reflect on their choices:

• "Did you make a good learning choice today? What made it good (or not)?"
• "Think about our learning goal. How do you think your choice helped you work toward that goal?"
• "If you got to do this same exercise again tomorrow, which choice would you make? Why?"
• "Do you think your choice allowed you to be in the 'just right' zone? How do you know?"

Review Learning

You can also help students review their work and learning, considering what went well and what could be better. Encourage students to think about the learning activity or work as a whole, or encourage them to think about specific attributes of their learning. By helping students accurately self-assess their work and learning, you help them better understand themselves as learners and consider their specific learning needs and preferences, which in turn will help them continue to develop the skills of metacognition that enable them to be more self-directed as learners.

• "What is one important thing you learned while working on this activity?"
• "Look back over your work and circle one problem you are proud of. Be ready to share with a partner why you are proud of that example."
• "What is one part of your work that went especially well for you today? What might have been better?"

Consider Goals

Effective and realistic goal-setting is a powerful skill you can help your students develop through the review stage of choice. Too often in schools today, all learning goals are set by the teacher or the curriculum—and posted at the front of the room before students have even begun the lesson. Though this is done because of a well-intentioned goal to help students be clear about the purpose of a learning task, if overdone, it may have the effect of distancing students from the learning. After all, if someone else is in charge of the learning goals, isn't the same person in charge of the work? Instead, you might consider ways for students to do more goal-setting. This can help strengthen student ownership and intrinsic motivation of work. Instead of telling them what they should work on, you're asking them, "What do you know about yourself as a learner? What do you think you need to work on next?" Goals can also help provide bridges from one part of an activity to another or from one lesson to the next, creating a more cohesive feel to work in general.

• "Yesterday, we examined figurative language in the books we're reading. Today, we're going to continue that work. Think about the goal that you set yesterday and how it might help you as a reader today."

• "Our learning goal as a class is to 'practice creating patterns.' What's a personal goal you have about creating patterns?"

• "Think about where you are with your writing piece right now. Set a realistic goal for the rest of the week. What do you hope to accomplish by Friday?"

• "We've worked hard at creating effective presentations—ones that are both active and interactive. What's a goal you have for the next time you give a presentation?"

• "On a Post-it note, jot down a goal for your writing tomorrow and place it in your writing journal as a reminder."

Review in Combination

Of course, there's no reason to limit ourselves to just one type of reflection. While it's wise not to overwhelm learners by asking them to engage in reviews that are overly complex and confusing, there are times you might want to help students review more than one aspect of their work at once. Students might both reflect on their learning and set a goal for the future. They might think about whether their choice helped them learn while also reviewing the depth of their learning.

• "Do you think you made a good choice during this class period? What information about the water cycle did your choice help you learn?"

• "What went well with your work today? What's a goal you have for tomorrow?"

• "Did your choice work for you as a learner today? How do you think it helped you work toward your learning goals? Which goal will you focus on next?"

Structures and Strategies to Help Students Review

Just as there is a wide variety of strategies to help students make good choices, there are many different ways to help them review their learning. In fact, many of the ideas offered for making good choices (partner chats, journal writing, silent reflection, etc.) work well as strategies to help students review and reflect. And just like with the "choose" phase of choice, the amount of time students spend reviewing their learning should be in proportion to the amount of time spent working. In a one-hour reading block in which there is a 10-minute focus lesson and 45 minutes for students to read, they might spend two minutes deciding which book will best help them practice the skill of the focus lesson and three minutes reviewing what they learned and how the book helped them practice. In a six-week engineering unit, in which students choose various structures to build and test, they might have several days to learn about various possible structures and then choose ones in which they are most interested, and then wrap up the unit by reflecting for one or more class periods on various phases and outcomes of the work.

Strategies for Reviewing Simple and Short Choice Activities

The following examples of strategies for helping students review simple or brief choice work can add to the ideas listed in the similar section of the "choose" chapter.

• **Fist-to-five.** Students show, on one hand (on a scale of zero to five fingers), how they would rate or rank an aspect of their work. "Using fist-to-five, show how hard you think you worked today. A fist means there was no effort at all, and a five means that you were pushing yourself to your limit."

• **Exit ticket.** In the last few minutes of a lesson or class period, have students write a sentence or two on an index card in which they reflect on an aspect of their work. For example, students might write to the prompt: "Agree or disagree with this statement and explain your thinking: 'My choice today helped me meet the lesson's learning targets.'"

• **Concentric circles.** Have students stand in two concentric circles, with the inside circle facing out and the outside circle facing in. Students partner with someone in the other circle and answer a question ("What was an aspect of your work you were proud of today?"). After a minute or two, shift the circles to form new partners and give another question ("What's a goal you have for tomorrow's work?").

• **Tweet it.** Have students answer a reflection question in 140 characters or less. Once they have composed their tweets, they might share them with others at their table or pass them in so you can check them all out.

• **Thumbs up, down, or to the side.** Students rate their thinking, work, or effort by showing a thumbs up for high or a thumbs down for low. Thumbs can be placed somewhere in between to show in-between ratings.

• **3-2-1.** Students respond to three prompts to self-evaluate. "Write three things you did well, two questions you have, and one thing you could do better next time."

• **Two roses and a thorn.** Students choose two things that went well (roses) and one that could be improved (thorn) and write a short reflection about each.

Strategies for Reviewing More Complex and Longer-Range Choice Review

Longer-range and more complex choice work merits deeper and more complex review strategies. Sometimes, you might want to build periodic reviews into larger projects. For example, if students are using a checklist to keep track of stages of an independent project, you might have students add a note in a designated space on the checklist page every few days to reflect on the progress they're making. Even with ongoing reflection, more substantial reviews can help students build a sense of pride in the accomplishments and help deepen their learning at the end of a complex project. Here are some more ideas for review strategies.

• **Rubrics.** Very often rubrics only include product or standards-based outcomes ("My story includes basic elements of a beginning, middle, and end" or "My story involves new and challenging Spanish vocabulary"). Consider including some process criteria as a part of rubrics. For example, "I worked well in my zone of proximal development."

• **Narratives.** Have students write a narrative at the conclusion of their work project. They might reflect on all three review criteria: the effectiveness of their choices, the substance of their learning, and goals for future work.

• **Video blogs.** Students can review their work through a video recording in which they explain what they learned, about both the content and themselves as learners, through their work. In projects that are displayed electronically, these video blogs make a nice conclusion!

Using Choice to Help Students Review

Sometimes, students might struggle with a particular type of review strategy, so you can use the strategy of choice to help all find a way of reflecting on their work that makes sense for them! For example, offer students two choices of exit tickets: "Share one or two things you learned through your choice activity today. You can either write a tweet or draw a cartoon sketch."

To be clear, this is *not* a time to engage in the full choose-do-review process of choice. You should certainly encourage students to make a thoughtful choice ("Think about which type of exit ticket will best help you share your thinking") and time to complete the work, but I would discourage you from having students review their review ("Think about the review strategy you used to review. How did that review strategy help you as a learner?" is carrying things a bit far!).

Is Sharing a Kind of Review?

A common question I hear from teachers is "Is sharing a kind of review?" For example, at the end of a reading period, teachers might have students share a bit about their book with a partner. Or, at the conclusion of a lab, students might give a brief oral summary of their experiment to the class. Similarly, at the end of independent research projects students might share their projects with the class or with a broader audience, such as a neighboring class or parents. Do these count as "review?"

It depends. A question I often respond with is, "Does the sharing help students engage in self-reflection?" Often, when students share work with a partner or with the whole class, the emphasis is on showing the work, not necessarily on self-reflection. In fact, sharing work often encourages other-reflection, where students focus on attributes of each other's work. That's not to say that's a bad thing—you can often learn a lot by hearing about someone else's learning, it just isn't about reviewing your own work.

After all, what's most important about the "review" stage of the process is that you're helping students learn to be more metacognitive—to understand themselves better as learners. Though sharing work might have many benefits (like reinforcing their memory of content and teaching other students), in order to help students deepen their thinking, the sharing should include explicitly reflective elements ("Share a bit about your book, and explain whether or not you would choose a book like this again"). You can also teach students how to ask questions of each other that encourage self-reflection ("What was something that you found challenging about this project?"), though I've found that these types of questions sometimes feel forced. In order to feel authentic and work well, students need lots of coaching and support.

Conclusion

It was late May, and my 5th grade students had just finished creating a movie based on the Lewis and Clark expedition. Students had all worked on various parts of the project, some of which were choice-based and some of which were assigned. Students had written the screenplay and scripts, designed scenery and costumes, and practiced and performed roles, and we had just held our first official viewing of the movie at an evening event for parents. The next day, we all filled out a review questionnaire to reflect on individual accomplishments as well as on the project as a whole. Students had interesting insights into the work they put in, the skills they had learned, and suggestions for making the project better if I tried it again with another class.

I also filled out one of the questionnaires. As a teacher, I wanted to make sure to take time to review and reflect on the work we had done as a class, as well as on my implementation of the project. What had I done well? What could I have done better? Just as our students grow and learn through reflection, so too can we, and this is the next and final step in our own teacher implementation process, and the subject of the next chapter.

CHAPTER 9

Professional Reflection

| Create Good Choices | → | Facilitate Student Choice: Choose, Do, Review | → | **Professional Reflection** |

One of my favorite books about teaching is a little gem of a book, *Sammy and His Behavior Problems*. In this book, 3rd grade teacher Caltha Crowe chronicles a year with a student who had particularly challenging behaviors. He was sweet and caring but could also explode unpredictably. He was smart and creative but often more intent on his own side projects than he was on the content of the class. He desperately wanted friends but struggled with the social skills needed to make and keep them. Caltha's book is filled with wonderfully practical, kind, and supportive techniques for helping students who struggle with behavior in the classroom, but this isn't why I love the book.

What I love most about this book are the excerpts from Caltha's diary that are sprinkled throughout the text. For as wonderful as the strategies that she suggests are, it's the *thinking behind the strategies* that is the real treasure in this book. Through these journal entries, readers get the rare treat of a glimpse into the thought process this master teacher uses to hone her practice, asking questions and wondering about next steps and strategies. You get to hear her celebrate successes and struggle with failures. Here's an excerpt, just to give you a taste:

From my journal, January 12: Complacency can become my nemesis if I'm not careful. Now, in January, it seems that Sammy has made so much progress since September. It would be easy to take this improvement for granted, yet I know I need to push myself to remember to congratulate him on his frequent successes. His self-control is still tenuous. It would be all too easy for him to fall back into old behaviors and patterns. My reinforcements are helping the new behaviors stick. No matter how tempted I am to breathe a sigh of relief and say, "Whew, that's done!" and focus on other things, I know if I start to do that, his efforts will begin to unravel. (Crowe, 2010, pp. 92–93)

Great teachers, like Caltha, are deeply reflective. Thinking about our practice—considering what went well and what could have been better—is how we grow as professionals. It's how you figure out what to keep, what to modify, and what to toss aside. Sometimes, it is through purposeful reflection that you uncover intuitive strategies that you didn't even know you used, enabling you to employ them with more intentionality. It is how to improve with experience so that you can lead great learning with your students and keep your passion for the profession high. And so, reflecting on the choices you offered students and your facilitation of the learning process in which they engaged is the crucial final step in the teacher's own three-part process.

As you examine effective reflection, consider these two important categories that this chapter will address: What should you reflect on so that you pay attention to what is most important, and what are some practical strategies for reflection that will fit into your daily lives as busy teachers?

About What Should You Reflect?

There are no hard and fast rules that I know of about what teachers should and shouldn't reflect on, but I do think that teachers sometimes inadvertently spend more time than necessary reflecting on some things (e.g., a phone call from one disgruntled parent) while not spending enough time focusing on others (e.g., whether or not the homework we assign is actually helping students learn). So, in that vein, I'd like to offer a few categories for reflection that are especially important to consider as you come to the end of a lesson, activity, or unit in which you've offered choices—categories that will most help you learn and grow.

Student Learning

This is the first and most important category to consider. Did students learn? How well did they learn? Do you think that choices helped students learn better? Which choices seemed to be best? When thinking about Christine and her sun project (in Chapter 5), I realized that the choices, as they were given, didn't work well to help her learning. While other students chose projects that supported their learning (scale drawings of the planets or a fictional story about walking on the planet Mars and describing the scenery), Christine's project did not. Moving forward, I paid closer attention to projects students wanted to take on, working to make sure there was a connection between the project and the content.

In another instance, I saw how choice helped. To practice multiplication facts, students chose between using flash cards, writing them over and over, and practicing skip counting. I remember watching a student who had practiced skip counting later on as he worked on a multi-digit multiplication problem. I saw him quickly counting by 7s to work out 7 x 6. He found a strategy that worked.

In particular, with learning that involves choice, ask a specific question about student learning: Did *all* students learn? Because one of the primary goals of offering choice is to help students self-differentiate their work, this is an important question. The whole class was working on multiplying fractions. Did students of all skill levels get to practice in their zones of proximal development? Which students seemed to self-differentiate well and who might need some extra coaching?

And finally, ask yourself about students' growth in their knowledge of themselves as learners. Did students learn something about themselves through the choices they made? When they reviewed their work, did they practice skills of metacognition and self-reflection? Are they learning how to be better learners?

Student Engagement

Closely related (one would hope!) to student learning is student engagement. How invested were students in their work? Were they going through the motions, just playing the school game, or were they really deeply interested in what they were doing? Were they surprised when you announced that it was time to wrap up? Did they groan at the end of the work session? Did anyone ask, "Can we please have a few more minutes?" Which choices were students most eager to try, and which ones did they not choose? Which students seemed to choose options that they found engaging, and which ones might need some extra help with finding a good match in the future? When students are engaged in work that is appropriately challenging and that they find enjoyable and satisfying, the tone of the room takes on an unmistakable, joyful quality. There's a buzz and hum of activity. Students' voices are cheerful and energetic.

Because one of the primary goals of choice is to boost student engagement, both by helping students find appropriately challenging work and through tapping into their interests and strengths, this is another important category to consider. Sometimes I have offered certain choices that I thought students would love only to find them ignored and unchosen. There have been other times when I've included a choice, not expecting many takers, only to see that option be the most popular. Why did that happen? What is it about some choices that seem to resonate, and why do others flop?

Management

Think about the way you facilitated the work. Were students able to choose efficiently and effectively? Did they have the materials they needed, and did they take care of the room while working? Were students able to work independently so that you could coach individuals and small groups? Did students have the right amount of time to choose, do, and review? What aspects of this work seemed to work particularly smoothly and which elements were bumpy? For example, perhaps students chose their work option thoughtfully and quickly but then had a hard time finding a good place to work. How might you facilitate that differently next time? Good classroom management is so much more than having students who are in control—it's about creating learning environments where students can devote most of their time and energy to learning.

How Should You Reflect?

Few would argue that teacher reflection is important—everyone knows that refining practice takes thoughtful reflection. The challenge is finding time to reflect and having systems for doing so efficiently and effectively.

To start, consider that the amount of time you spent reflecting on a given assignment or project should be proportional to the breadth and depth of the work. After a 30-minute choice activity, you may reflect as you walk down the hall, "Hmmm. That went pretty well. Most students were engaged and enjoyed the three choices I gave. A few were getting restless towards the end. Maybe next time I can find an option that involves more movement." After a semester-long, cross-department, multi-genre community service venture, you'll likely want to sit down for several hours with your colleagues, surfacing successes and challenges, sifting through student feedback, and charting and recording ideas to shape planning for next year.

With that in mind, let's explore a few specific vehicles for reflecting effectively and efficiently on your facilitation of choice.

Student Work

Very often, one of the best ways to reflect on the effectiveness of student learning and engagement is by looking at student work. For example, at the end of a writing period in which students were beginning rough drafts of personal narratives, you might have all students use Post-it notes to designate their starting and ending points of the period's writing. You could spend five minutes, flipping through journals and glancing at their writing. How much did students write? Did they all have a topic that they could start? From your brief glances, how strong are the initial drafts? Are there a few students who you should make sure to touch base with tomorrow? By pulling the journals of the few students who need a check-in, you have now created your touch-base group for tomorrow's writing period.

Sometimes, reviewing student work can feel time-consuming. Especially when reviewing daily work as you look for general trends and themes, consider having students note where you should focus. For example, at the end of a math period where students have been practicing a variety of problems, you might announce, "Everyone, take a green colored pencil and circle a problem about which you feel confident—one that you're pretty sure is solid. Then use a blue pencil to circle one that felt shaky—one that you struggled with or that you aren't sure is correct." This then serves as a way for students to review their work while also allowing you to be efficient with your time as you reflect on their learning and progress.

Self-Reflection

There are many strategies to use for reflecting on your own. What's most important is that you find something that works for you. Ideally, the strategy gives you an opportunity to both think and keep track of that thinking so it can help you adjust your practice in the future.

• **Journaling.** Like Caltha, you could keep an ongoing journal. You might try free-writing, letting your thoughts and reflections wander, or you might give yourself specific prompts, such as, "What was something that went well today?" Try carving out specific times each day when you will write. Even just 10 minutes a day of reflecting through writing will yield a powerful and rich trove of insights and information over time.

• **Internal dialogue.** One of my favorite methods of self-reflection is talking to myself. As a general rule, it's best to do this internally (especially when in public), though I have been caught talking to myself in the car. (Fortunately, with the advent of Bluetooth technology, passersby probably assume I'm on the phone.) Like journaling, it's important to give yourself a structure. Perhaps you like to think while you exercise or during your commute. You might steal away a few quiet moments in the classroom when students are at lunch. Make sure that you have a place to jot down notes when you think of something you want to remember.

• **Blogging.** I know several avid bloggers, and they've all said the same thing. They enjoy sharing blogs, but their primary reason for blogging is personal reflection and growth. So if you are excited to use choice more frequently and intentionally, what about starting a blog about your journey? Try writing one entry a week where you share some of your challenges, successes, insights, and questions. This will serve as a steady ongoing reflection format and will also allow you to look back over time at trends and personal growth.

Collaborative Reflection

I almost always learn more deeply when engaged with others. Having to articulate my thinking to share with others, asking questions, and hearing about others' experiences and perspectives help me reflect more powerfully. There's also a certain level of accountability that comes with collaborative conversations. When sharing ideas and thinking with colleagues, it's somehow easier to move forward and try new things.

• **Ask a colleague to observe.** Invite a colleague into your room to observe a lesson—or even just part of an activity—and ask for feedback. "What did you think of the choices I gave? How engaged did my students seem to you?" Keeping collegial observations light and informal can help lower the anxiety you may feel about having someone watch you teach. It can also make them easier to schedule, because you all can probably carve out 5 or 10 minutes to visit a colleague's classroom.

• **Host a team talk.** When a team of teachers works together on a common challenge, great collaborative thinking can happen. I've worked with teams of teachers all implementing choice intentionally, and I'm always amazed by the creative power that is unleashed when teachers reflect together. Sometimes, a grade level team might implement a common choice project together, generating ideas for a great collaborative project. I've also seen teachers benefit from working with diverse colleagues, who teach different content at different grade levels. Sometimes, not being immersed in content is freeing and allows people to share ideas that are more creative.

• **Engage in an online community.** Another way to connect with colleagues to engage in reflection about choice is through meeting with others online. You might form a private Facebook group with a few colleagues from other schools or districts. Or you might find (or create!) a Twitter chat group that meets once a week to discuss your implementation of choice. Connecting with colleagues from diverse settings allows you to reflect on different kinds of questions and challenges.

• **Ask your students.** Liz Olbrych's students at Staples High School, in Westport, Connecticut, had just finished a semester-long at-home exploration of film and the film industry through a wide range of open-ended choices, all of which reinforced content and themes from class. Liz was impressed with the quality of students' work and wanted to hear some of their opinions about the project. Many expressed enjoyment of the work, and several suggested she tighten up guidelines a bit to make it easier to understand. Liz was able to reflect about her work in new ways through talking with her students. Students, after all, are perhaps one of your most valuable resources for your own professional development—for no one knows your teaching strengths and challenges better!

Conclusion

When non-educator friends of mine ask me about the most important attributes of a good teacher, there are several that come to mind. Good teachers are kind, supportive, smart, and thoughtful, and perhaps above all, they find deep and immense pleasure in working with their students. None of these are a surprise to anyone. There's one quality that I state that occasionally raises eyebrows, as if it's one they hadn't before considered: Great teachers are great learners. After all, can you imagine a football coach who doesn't know how to play football or a dance instructor who doesn't dance?

As Pete Hall and Alisa Simeral state in their book *Teach, Reflect, Learn*, "Growth, improvement, progress, and development don't just happen overnight, and they typically don't happen accidentally. They're a result of intentionality, planning, conscious effort, and thought" (2015, p. 14). It is through intentional reflection that you will continue to grow and learn every time you use choice with your students.

Conclusion

In times of change learners inherit the earth; while the learned find themselves beautifully equipped to deal with a world that no longer exists.

— Eric Hoffer

The above quote hung by the entrance of Flanders Elementary School in East Lyme, Connecticut, where I had my first teaching job, right out of college. Every morning for the first six years of my career, I was greeted with this reminder about the true purpose of education. In many ways, I see choice as one of our most crucial tools to help create students who are true learners—people who take charge of their own learning, understand themselves as learners, and see a need to find personal relevance, challenge, and joy in daily work. Through empowering our students and helping them learn how to learn, we will help shape people who can find meaningful careers and seek pleasure in the act of growing and learning for the rest of their lives.

If you've made it this far into this book, chances are, you're in agreement. Yet, it can be a bit daunting to know where to start. After all, choice can be used in so many different ways in nearly every content area that it can be overwhelming. So, with that in mind, I'd like to offer a few suggestions that might help you get started.

• **If you're new to choice, start small.** Just as you need to scaffold your use of choice for students who haven't yet had much experience with it, also give yourself permission to go slowly. For example, you might first offer your students the choice of whether to work on an activity alone or with a partner.

Or try a different kind of simple choice. Let students decide whether crayons, colored pencils, or markers are the best tool for coloring in their graphs. Give students the choice between two articles to read or two worksheets to try. Regardless of the kind of choice you offer, have students engage in the full choose-do-review process and see how it goes. Then, try that same kind (or one very similar) of choice again the next day. Then, try it again. Force yourself to engage in the three-part teacher process, where you think about good choices, facilitate the full choose-do-review process for students, and then reflect about how it all went.

• **If you're ready, try different or more complex choice.** Perhaps you already use choice with students. How could you challenge yourself to try something a bit more complex? A 3rd grade teacher who already lets students choose books to read might challenge himself to give choices in math. A 7th grade social studies teacher who lets students choose research topics but then has all students create the same projects could run a class brainstorming session where students generate different kinds of projects they might create. A high school calculus teacher who has given students choice in class might decide to experiment with giving students choices with homework—helping students find appropriate practice exercises that fit their needs and schedules.

• **If you already give lots of choice, deepen your thinking about the process.** It might be that you offer students lots of choices throughout the day but rarely give students enough time to make good choices or review their learning after an activity. Maybe you've noticed that your choices feel uninspired or disconnected from learning goals. If so, you might focus on creating good choices for students—deepening your thinking about which choices will best suit the content, your students, and your logistics. Perhaps you find that choice sometimes feels contrived. Are there times you give choice when perhaps you shouldn't? Don't forget that choice is best when used with intentionality. Why are you giving choice? Is it to boost engagement through self-differentiation or to connect with students' interests, needs, and strengths? Remember that choice is a means to an end, not an end in and of itself!

• **Remember to consider strategies that will boost the effectiveness of choice.** Whether you are brand new to choice or have been using choice as a learning strategy for years, there are likely ways you can help students better engage with choice. How could you continue to build a positive community of learners—where students feel safe enough to take the risks needed to make choices that are personally engaging? How can you increase students' sense of ownership of their work so they are doing their work and not yours? What skills of metacognition would help your students make better choices—ones that are reflective of their understanding of themselves as learners?

And finally, let's remember that one of the great benefits of using choice with our students is selfish. When our students are more fully engaged in learning; when they are learning more; when our classrooms are vibrant, safe, and joyful learning environments; and when students look forward to coming to school each day, we have more fun. We can have more moments where we remember why we came to teaching in the first place—because we find immense joy and pleasure in leading great learning.

Planning Guide and Sample Plans

In the pages that follow, you will find a few resources to help you as you work to integrate more choices for students into your lessons and units. The first is a blank planning guide. I suggest using it as a starting point and creating your own, modifying it to suit your particular style and the structure of the work you are planning.

There are also several examples of plans that are filled in to give you some ideas about how you might use the planning template efficiently and effectively. I've included plans from across grade levels and content areas, as well as examples of varying length and complexity. I hope you find these inspirational and helpful.

Choice Planning Sheet

Topic/Goal:

Good Choices: List many possibilities, then circle or mark the ones you'll use. Remember, good choices should match your curricular **goals,** your **students,** and your **logistics!**

Student Process:		
Choose	**Do**	**Review**
How will you help students make choices that match their needs/interests?	What will you do to support students as they work?	How will you facilitate students' thinking about their choices/work after they finish?

Teacher Reflection: After this choice experience, reflect on what went well and what could have been better. Note ideas to remember for the future.

Grade 2: Literacy, Fables, and Folktales

Topic/Goal: *Students will explore the central message and morals of fables and folktales through a reader's theatre experience. They will also practice reading aloud with fluency, accuracy, and expression.*

Good Choices: List many possibilities, then circle or mark the ones you'll use. Remember, good choices should match your curricular **goals,** your **students,** and your **logistics**!

Students will choose either one of the fables and folktales in the class literature anthology (The Tortoise and the Hare, Paul Bunyan, *or* Stone Soup) *or a Dr. Seuss title* (Horton Hatches the Egg, The Lorax, *or* The Butter Battle Book).

Student Process:		
Choose (2 days)	**Do (1–2 weeks)**	**Review (5–10 min.)**
How will you help students make choices that match their needs/ interests?	What will students do? What will you do to support students as they work?	How will you facilitate students' thinking about their choices/ work?
Structure/Process: • *I will read each book aloud to the class over the course of two days. Students will be told ahead of time that they will choose one to explore more deeply.* • *Students will then get a paper with all six stories in a list. They will place a 1-2-3 next to their top three choices. I will try and give them one of their top two choices.* Language to Use: • *"As you listen to these stories, think about ones that you would like to get to know really well—and ones that would be fun to practice reading and performing!"*	Students: • *In small groups, students will practice reading their stories. They will practice reading with fluency and expression. Students will also practice reading on their own.* • *Students will, as a group, decide what the moral or message of the story is. They will all practice articulating this message.* • *Students will create simple cut-out figures and scenery to support the story.* • *Students will practice reading their stories and using props to create a performance.* • *Students will perform their story for the class.*	Structure/Process: • *Students will each confer with me during reading workshop. I'll tailor each conference to the needs and strengths of each student.* Language to Use (examples): • *"Think about the story you chose. Do you think it provided a fun challenge for you as a reader?"* • *"What are some ways you improved as a reader from this work?"* • *"Were you happy with the choice you made? Is there another story that you also would have enjoyed?"*

• *"Now, think about which stories would be fun for you to practice reading and perform in a reader's theatre. Think about ones that will give you a fun challenge as a reader!"*	Teacher: • *I will meet with each group to help them practice and coach them as they find a moral. This will happen during reading workshop.* • *I will confer with students individually to coach and support.* • *I will decide when each group is ready to perform.* • *Students' SPED and remedial support staff will help students throughout their work.*	

Teacher Reflection: After this choice experience, how will you reflect on what went well and what could have been better?

I'll use our standards-based rubric that we developed as a grade level to assess students' accuracy, fluency, expression, and articulation of morals and messages. This will help me reflect on how this work helped develop students' skills. I will also have our school's literacy coach join us for some of the work and ask her for advice to give me ideas for future reader's theatres.

Grade 5, Math

Topic/Goal: *Students will practice the standard multiplication algorithm.*

Good Choices: List many possibilities, then circle or mark the ones you'll use. Remember, good choices should match your curricular **goals,** your **students,** and your **logistics**!

regular worksheet ~~Show Me (app)~~ ~~manipulatives~~ ~~playing cards~~

~~dice~~ worksheet: blank worksheet
correct mistakes (make up own problems)

~~computer program~~

Student Process:		
Choose (2 min.)	**Do (30 min.)**	**Review (3 min.)**
How will you help students make choices that match their needs/interests?	What will students do? What will you do to support students as they work?	How will you facilitate students' thinking about their choices/work?
Structure/Process: • *Private reflection* • *Write why choosing (in just a few words)*	Students: • *Work independently* • *Sit in regular work spots* • *Support/coach each other*	Structure/Process: • *Short written explanation* • *On own, private reflection*
Language to Use: • *"Find a 'just right' choice."* • *"Which do you think would help push your thinking?"* • *"Ask yourself: 'Do I understand this well enough to be successful?'"*	Teacher: • *Circulate and coach* • *Students will raise hands to get help.* • *May sit at back table with group if needed.*	Language to Use: • *"How did your choice help you practice?"*

Teacher Reflection: After this choice experience, how will you reflect on what went well and what could have been better?

I'll review students' writing from both "choose" and "review" phases to look at their thinking. This may help me consider new ways to help them make good choices.

Grade 7, World Language, Spanish

Topic/Goal: *Students will understand the importance of Día de los Muertos (and differentiate it from Halloween) and will create a project (in Spanish) to showcase what they learn.*

Good Choices: List many possibilities, then circle or mark the ones you'll use. Remember, good choices should match your curricular **goals,** your **students,** and your **logistics**!

Possible Projects: *picture book, ~~PowerPoint, Prezi, make a video,~~ poster, ~~recipes, lists of foods,~~ comic, essay, song/poem*

Rationale: *Dealing with technology will make this too complicated—especially for a short project. The recipes and lists of foods aren't central enough to the core content.*

Student Process:		
Choose (1 class period)	**Do (3 class periods)**	**Review (1 class period)**
How will you help students make choices that match their needs/interests?	What will students do? What will you do to support students as they work?	How will you facilitate students' thinking about their choices/work?
Structure/Process: • *Students will first learn about Día de los Muertos through a short video and class discussion. All will fill out a Venn diagram to differentiate it from Halloween.* • *Students will be encouraged to choose a project that works with their strengths.* • *They will write down their strengths on a card and discuss with partners before choosing.* Language to Use: • *"Choose a project that connects with your strengths. For example, if you enjoy drawing, you might create a poster or picture book."*	Students: • *Use materials available in classroom* • *Work both in and out of classroom as needed (out of class optional)* • *Okay to finish with in-process work if time runs out* • *Students will share in small groups.* Teacher: • *Coach, especially keep students on task and chatting in Spanish (not English)* • *Encourage students to support and help each other*	Structure/Process: • *Students will examine work to decide . . .* Language to Use: • *"What did you learn?"* • *"How did this project help your learning?"* • *"Did you enjoy your choice? Would you choose differently next time?"*

Teacher Reflection: After this choice experience, how will you reflect on what went well and what could have been better?

I'll look at students' projects and listen as they share in small groups to determine how much they learned. I'll watch for engagement to see which choices seemed to be best. I may ask students what other choices I might offer next year.

Grade 11, Ecology: Interdependent Relationships in Ecosystems

Topic/Goal: *Students will begin to explore some basic information and ask some initial questions about the interdependence of relationships in ecosystems. This class period will serve as a kickoff for the course.*

Good Choices: List many possibilities, then circle or mark the ones you'll use. Remember, good choices should match your curricular **goals,** your **students,** and your **logistics**!

Students will choose to find examples of interdependent relationships within species (wolves working together), examples of cross-species interdependence (bees/flowers), or examples of interdependent relationships between humans and other species. These examples will serve as a starting point for asking questions that the class will explore.

Student Process:		
Choose (1 min.)	**Do (30 min.)**	**Review (3 min.)**
How will you help students make choices that match their needs/interests?	What will students do? What will you do to support students as they work?	How will you facilitate students' thinking about their choices/work?
Structure/Process:	Students:	Structure/Process:
• *Students will hear an example of each type of interdependent relationship for which they might find examples.*	• *All students will record examples on a note-taking sheet.*	• *Students will reflect on a question with their table group.*
• *Students may either work on their own or with others exploring the same topic.*	• *If students work together, one note-taking sheet can be used for both students.*	Language to Use:
• *Students may use either print resources in classroom or one of several websites given to find different examples.*	Teacher:	• *"Look at the list of examples you found. What's one that was new for you—one you didn't already know?"*
	• *I will circulate and listen to students' conversations (and observe their note taking). This will help me begin to assess what students already know.*	
	• *If students are having a hard time coming up with examples, I'll help lead them to a resource that might help.*	

Language to Use:	• *After 15 minutes of note taking, we'll share ideas together to generate a class list (with columns for each category).*	
• *"Think about which of these topics you're most interested in exploring. Each will be added to a class list that will help drive our questions for this unit."*		

Teacher Reflection: After this choice experience, how will you reflect on what went well and what could have been better?

I'm interested to see how well students can sustain interest in one animal, so I'm going to watch energy levels as the week goes on. I'll also use the written reflections that students give to better understand how they felt about the work. I wonder how well they'll be able to articulate whether they made a good choice or not.

References

Anderson, M. (2010). *The well-balanced teacher: How to work smarter and stay sane inside the classroom and out.* Alexandria, VA: ASCD.

Anderson, M., & Dousis, A. (2006.) *The research-ready classroom: Differentiating instruction across content areas.* Portsmouth, NH: Heinemann.

Brady, K., Forton, M. B., & Porter, D. 2010. *Rules in school: Teaching discipline in the responsive classroom.* Turners Falls, MA: Northeast Foundation for Children.

Center for Responsive Schools. (2015). *The first six weeks of school* (2nd ed.). Turners Falls, MA: Center for Responsive Schools.

Crain, W. (2011). *Theories of development: Concepts and applications* (6th ed.). Upper Saddle River, NJ: Prentice Hall.

Crowe, C. (2010). *Sammy and his behavior problems: Stories and strategies from a teacher's year.* Turners Falls, MA: Northeast Foundation for Children.

Deci, E., with Flaste, R. (1995). *Why we do what we do: Understanding self-motivation.* New York: Penguin.

Denton, P. (2005). *Learning through academic choice.* Turners Falls, MA: Northeast Foundation for Children.

Denton, P. (2014). *The power of our words: Teacher language that helps children learn* (2nd ed.). Turners Falls, MA: Northeast Foundation for Children.

Dweck, C. (2006). *Mindset: The new psychology of success.* New York: Random House.

Dweck, C. (2007). The perils and promise of praise. *Educational Leadership, 65*(2), 34–39.

Frey, N., Fisher, D., & Everlove, S. (2009). *Productive group work: How to engage students, build teamwork, and promote understanding.* Alexandria, VA: ASCD.

Ginott, H. G. (1972). *Teacher and child: A book for parents and teachers.* New York: Macmillan.

Hall, P., & Simeral, A. (2015). *Teach, reflect, learn: Building your capacity for success in the classroom.* Alexandria, VA: ASCD.

Hattie, J., & Yates, G. C. R. (2014). *Visible learning and the science of how we learn.* New York: Routledge.

Jensen, E. (2005). *Teaching with the Brain in Mind* (2nd ed). Alexandria, VA: ASCD.

Johnson, S. (2010a, July). Steven Johnson: Where good ideas come from [Video file]. Retrieved from http://www.ted.com/talks/steven_johnson_where_good_ideas_come_from?language=en

Johnson, S. (2010b). *Where good ideas come from: The natural history of innovation.* New York: Riverhead Books.

Kohn, A. (1993). *Punished by rewards: The trouble with gold stars, incentive plans, A's, praise, and other bribes.* New York: Houghton Mifflin.

Lieber, C. L. (2009). *Getting classroom management right: Guided discipline in secondary schools.* Cambridge, MA: Educators for Social Responsibility.

Moll, L. C. (1990). *Vygotsky and education: Instructional implications and applications of sociohistorical psychology.* New York: Cambridge University Press.

Pearson, C. L., & Moomaw, W. (2005). The relationship between teacher autonomy and stress, work satisfaction, empowerment, and professionalism. *Educational Research Quarterly 29*(1), 37–53.

Pink, D. H. (2009). *Drive: The surprising truth about what motivates us.* New York: Riverhead Books.

Robinson, K. (2013, April). Ken Robinson: Escaping education's death valley [Video file]. Retrieved from http://www.ted.com/talks/ken_robinson_how_to_escape_education_s_death_valley?language=en

Schlender, B., & Tetzeli, R. (2015). *Becoming Steve Jobs: The evolution of a reckless upstart into a visionary leader.* New York: Crown Publishing Group.

Willis, J. (2006). *Research-based strategies to ignite student learning.* Alexandria, VA: ASCD.

Wood, C. (2007). *Yardsticks: Children in the classroom ages 4–14* (3rd ed.). Turners Falls, MA: Northeast Foundation for Children.

Index

The letter *f* following a page number denotes a figure.

About the Author

Mike Anderson has been an educator for more than 20 years. An elementary school teacher for 15 years, he has also taught preschool and university graduate level classes. He spent many years as a presenter, consultant, author, and developer for Northeast Foundation for Children, a nonprofit organization dedicated to helping create safe, joyful, and challenging classrooms and schools. In 2004 Mike was awarded a national Milken Educator Award, and in 2005 he was a finalist for New Hampshire Teacher of the Year.

Now, as an education consultant, Mike works with schools in rural, urban, and suburban settings across the United States. He has also taught workshops and presented at conferences in Canada and Mexico. Mike supports teachers and schools on a wide variety of topics: embedding choice in everyday learning, blending social-emotional and academic teaching, using respectful and effective discipline strategies, staying healthy and balanced as an educator, and many more.

Mike is the author of many books about great teaching and learning including *The Research-Ready Classroom* (Heinemann, 2006), *The Well-Balanced Teacher* (ASCD, 2010), and *The First Six Weeks of School, 2nd Edition* (CRS, 2015). His articles have been published in various resources including *Educational Leadership*, *Language Arts*, Teach.com, and EdCircuit. He has been a guest on Bam! Radio, EduTalk Radio, and the Re:Teaching podcast from the Teacher Learning Sessions. Recently, he served as an ASCD Whole Child advisor. He also writes frequently on his personal blog through his website.

Mike lives in Durham, New Hampshire, with his incredible wife Heather, who is also an educator. Together, they co-teach the most challenging and rewarding class they have ever had, comprised of their two independent and curious children, Ethan and Carly, and their somewhat anxious and totally adorable dog, Olive.

To learn more about Mike and his work, visit his website: www.leadinggreat learning.com. You can also follow him on Twitter at @balancedteacher.

Related ASCD Resources

At the time of publication, the following ASCD resources were available (ASCD stock numbers appear in parentheses). For up-to-date information about ASCD resources, go to www.ascd.org. You can search the complete archives of *Educational Leadership* at http://www.ascd.org/el.

ASCD EDge®

Exchange ideas and connect with other educators interested in various topics, including literacy, on the social networking site ASCD EDge® at http://ascdedge.ascd.org/

Print Products

The Well Balanced Teacher: How to Work Smarter and Stay Sane Inside the Classroom and Out by Mike Anderson (#111004)

Breaking Free from Myths About Teaching and Learning: Innovation as an Engine for Student Success by Allison Zmuda (#109041)

The Classroom of Choice: Giving Students What They Need and Getting What You Want by Jonathan C. Erwin (#104020)

Real Engagement: How do I help my students become motivated, confident, and self-directed learners? (ASCD Arias) by Allison Zmuda and Robyn R. Jackson (#SF115056)

Teach, Reflect, Learn: Building Your Capacity for Success in the Classroom by Pete Hall and Alisa Simeral (#115040)

For more information: send e-mail to member@ascd.org; call 1-800-933-2723 or 703-578-9600, press 2; send a fax to 703-575-5400; or write to Information Services, ASCD, 1703 N. Beauregard St., Alexandria, VA 22311-1714 USA.

WHOLE CHILD
TENETS

 HEALTHY
Each student enters school healthy and learns about and practices a healthy lifestyle.

SAFE
Each student learns in an environment that is physically and emotionally safe for students and adults.

ENGAGED
Each student is actively engaged in learning and is connected to the school and broader community.

 SUPPORTED
Each student has access to personalized learning and is supported by qualified, caring adults.

CHALLENGED
Each student is challenged academically and prepared for success in college or further study and for employment and participation in a global environment.

THE **WHOLE CHILD**

ASCD's Whole Child approach is an effort to transition from a focus on narrowly defined academic achievement to one that promotes the long-term development and success of all children. Through this approach, ASCD supports educators, families, community members, and policymakers as they move from a vision about educating the whole child to sustainable, collaborative actions.

Learning to Choose, Choosing to Learn:
The Key to Student Motivation and Achievement relates to the **engaged**, **supported**, and **challenged** tenets.

For more about the Whole Child approach, visit
www.wholechildeducation.org.

LEARN. TEACH. LEAD.